the
VIDEO POKER
EDGE

How to Play Smart and Bet Right

Linda BOYD

SQUAREONE
GAMING GUIDES

This book, which contains the ideas and opinions of its author, is both educational and recreational in nature. It offers accurate and appropriate information regarding casino gambling; however, neither the publisher nor the author guarantee specific gaming outcomes. As a recreational pursuit, legalized casino gambling can be a source of great enjoyment. If, however, it becomes compulsive or addictive, don't hesitate to seek counseling. Help is available:

National Council on Problem Gambling, Inc.
24-Hour Confidential National Hotline:
1-800-522-4700
Website: www.ncpgambling.org/

Gamblers Anonymous
Website:
www.gamblersanonymous.org/

Cover Designer: Jeannie Tudor
Cover Photograph: Reprinted courtesy of IGT
Interior Graphics and Typesetting: Gary A. Rosenberg
Editor: Joanne Abrams

Square One Publishers
115 Herricks Road
Garden City Park, NY 11040
877-900-BOOK
www.squareonepublishers.com

Library of Congress Cataloging-in-Publication Data

Boyd, Linda.
  The video poker edge : how to play smart and bet right / Linda Boyd.
    p. cm.
  Includes index.
  ISBN 0-7570-0252-8 (pbk.)
 1. Video poker. 2. Gambling. I. Title.

GV1469.35.P65B68   2006
795.4120285—dc22

                           2005035957

Printed in the United States of America

10 9 8 7 6 5 4 3 2 1

CONTENTS

A NOTE ON GENDER

Video poker is enjoyed by men and women alike. Similarly, both men and women can be found working in all areas of a casino. To avoid long and awkward phrasing within sentences, but still acknowledge players and personnel of both genders, the publisher has chosen to alternate the use of male and female pronouns according to chapter. Therefore, odd-numbered chapters use male pronouns when referring to the third-person player or casino staff member, while even-numbered chapters employ female pronouns.

ACKNOWLEDGMENTS

I spent over four years asking questions of slot club managers, mechanics, bench technicians, slot technicians, casino hosts and hostesses, and anybody else with relevant information. I can't thank all of those by name who patiently answered my nosy questions, but I truly appreciate the enlightenment they provided.

Darrell Clasby—head technician at the Ramada Express in Laughlin, Nevada—allowed an interview on his own time and provided important information about the way video poker machines work. There were many others whose names I don't have or who want to remain anonymous for various reasons, but who cleared up common myths about the game.

I learned a lot by visiting the Slot Tech and Bench Tech forums online (www.delphiforums.com) and by talking to many mechanics and technicians. I thank them all.

I want to give special thanks to Bill Rodrigues, technician extraordinaire, who gave me almost unlimited access to his stories. Bill is living proof that the adage "There's no such thing as a dumb question" doesn't apply only in classrooms. He gave serious consideration, and of course, intelligent, well-informed answers, to what must have been some bizarre questions.

Seth Briliant, Senior Counsel for the New Jersey Casino Control Commission, shed some light on the legal issues related to video lottery terminals (VLTs).

I. Nelson Rose, one of the top legal authorities on gaming in the country, and Professor of Law at Wittier Law School, also took time to answer my questions.

The *Las Vegas Review-Journal* and *Las Vegas Sun* were both a wealth of knowledge on a wide range of topics, and have some of the top gaming experts in the world on their staff. (John L. Smith, in particular, is a paragon of knowledge on "all things Vegas.") The American Gaming Association's annual *State of the States Report* provided the details on exactly who is playing, as well as the various venues that have the games.

I spent hours researching everything I could find in print on the topic of video poker. My local Barnes & Noble as well as Borders bookstores allowed me to read for as long as I wanted in their stores—I purchased some books and passed on others—without a complaint.

Both the former and current moderators of vpFREE are patient souls who do so much, all gratis, to improve the overall knowledge of everything related to video poker. I have learned a lot from the 6,000-plus members.

I want to thank my publisher, Rudy Shur, for his amazing patience as I kept saying, "Just one more thing," and moaning over computer viruses, worms, and parasites. Joanne Abrams, my excellent editor, kept me focused on the topic and let me know when anything was the least bit confusing. It was often difficult for me to make a topic I'm so close to simple enough for other players, including novices. Without Joanne, I could not have done it.

I thank my nongambling sister, Eileen, who was a good sport and allowed herself to be dragged into various casinos so that she could use my strategy cards. She even put up with my yelling about penalty cards and exceptions. Thank you, Barbara, my close friend and willing gambling cohort, for the great times and many laughs we've shared on our casino forays—spanning over twenty-five years! I appreciate David, my nephew, the last Mohegan at the Full-Pay Deuces Wild and Full-Pay Joker Poker machines in Laughlin's Golden Nugget. We've had many years of fun playing just about every game in the casino. I guess you could say I'm a bad influence.

Of course, I appreciate the support from my husband, Thom, who was not born with a deck of cards in his hand and the word "Deal" on his forehead.

I'm sure I left a lot of people out, but to anybody who answered questions, letters, or emails: I am very grateful for your help.

If there are any errors in this book, they are my fault and not the mistakes of the experts who were so generous in giving me their time.

PREFACE

I am a former high school math teacher who always spent way too much of my spare time playing live table poker and blackjack. Several years ago, I became attracted to the fast play of video poker, and now I spend way too much time playing and analyzing the virtual games!

From the start, I was sure that there was a correct way to play every dealt hand, but I was frustrated over my inability to find a mathematically accurate strategy. I asked questions of others, mostly fellow players, and my confusion grew with the number of different responses I received. Further, many of the things I heard made absolutely no sense at all! I knew that statements like, "The machine tries to fool you, so you have to fool it back," or, "You're not getting Four of a Kind because you play too fast (or too slow)," were ridiculous.

I spent a lot of time in bookstores and online searching for basic video poker rules that were parallel to basic blackjack or craps strategies. I became a shameless "lurker" in video poker players' groups. (Through reading the posts, I learned a great deal about what's important to most players and what's simply too much information.)

My efforts to find a simple strategy, however, failed for a number of reasons. In blackjack, for example, a player decides how much to bet and whether to hit or stand based on a combination of card counting and basic blackjack strategy. Video poker is much more complicated, because there are far too many different games to allow use of the same "basic" strategy for every game.

The strategy tables I found were incorrect, incomprehensible due to their complexity, or too time-consuming to be practical. The mathematically correct way to play any dealt hand is based on the stated payout table in conjunction with statistical probabilities. In fact, even minor changes in the pay table can change the way a dealt hand should be played. If the only thing you do is to check the stated payout table before playing, and choose the highest payback for a given game, you will play longer on the same bankroll.

Using my husband, former students, and friends as guinea pigs, I field-tested many prototypes before choosing format options for my strategy cards. Although I originally had three different types of strategy cards—"Best Bets," "Taboos," and "Key Play"—I eventually combined the formats to create single easy-to-use cards that you can take with you to the casino. You'll find these removable strategy cards in the back of this book. The book itself not only presents these crucial strategies in more detail than the cards allow, but also provides all the information you need to know before you even sit down at the video poker machine. You see, over the years I learned that people too often make poor decisions when choosing a casino, selecting a game, or deciding on a particular machine. If you want the winning edge in video poker, you have to make a series of smart choices long before you pull out your strategy cards. In fact, if you choose the wrong machine, even the best strategies won't be of help to you.

Do I guarantee that you will win every time you play video poker? Absolutely not! My goal in both developing the strategy cards and writing this book was to substantially increase the amount of play on your bankroll, help you get your money's worth during your casino visits, and dispel myths surrounding the technical aspects of video poker. I invite and welcome your comments on my system, and wish you the best of luck in all your video poker-playing adventures.

INTRODUCTION

It wasn't that long ago when gamblers were mostly cigar-chomping men playing poker around a table in a smoke-filled room. Things have definitely changed! Today, casino players represent a cross-section of lifestyles, ages, races, and genders. Recent data from the American Gaming Association indicates that there is no stereotypical portrait of a "gambler." In fact, to meet the demands of a population that seems fascinated with the gambling experience, more and more casinos are under construction—throughout the United States and around the world.

Of all the gaming options available, the most popular is that of video poker. It is so popular, in fact, that the current trend is for casinos to remove table games to make more room for video poker machines. Why do so many players love video poker? A few reasons come to mind:

❏ Video poker is similar to regular poker, so the basic rules are familiar to many players.

❏ Video poker is fast-paced and exciting.

❏ Video poker gives players the opportunity to make decisions. Your skill in playing the cards will definitely affect the outcome of the game.

❏ Video poker offers the possibility of a large payoff.

❏ Video poker is one of the few casino options that, in some circumstances, offers player advantage games, giving *you* the edge over the casino!

If some video poker games give players the advantage, and players can use skill to affect the outcome of the game, you may wonder why every gambler isn't going home with piles of money. The answer is twofold. First, most players don't make a careful choice of casinos, games, and machines because they don't understand how important these decisions are. Second, even a player advantage game requires perfect or near-perfect play in order to win, and most people base their moves on guesswork and "commonsense" rather than proven strategies. You see, like any casino game that allows player interaction, beneath the neon lights and cacophony of sounds is the very logical field of probability and statistics. Regardless of some people's claims about lucky charms, "hot" machines, and winning streaks, the only way to win at video poker is to play according to the laws of mathematics.

By picking up this book, you have taken the first step toward gaining the winning edge in video poker. Each chapter will provide more of the information you need to make the smart decisions that separate the savvy video poker player from the average player—the person who bets on hunches and quickly loses his bankroll.

Chapter 1 begins by explaining the basics of video poker, comparing and contrasting it to table poker so that you understand both the similarities and the differences. Perhaps most important, this chapter introduces you to the eight video poker games I recommend because of their wide availability, their good returns, and their easy-to-use strategies. In each case, you'll be acquainted with the fundamentals of the game, as well as the best-paying version—the one you should look for when entering a casino.

An understanding of the video poker machine is essential if you're to play the game wisely and well. Chapter 2 covers the basics of using the machine, warns you against some common mistakes, and explains the workings of the random number generator—the internal computer that allows you to participate in the playing of the game. This chapter also debunks some common video poker myths and provides detailed information on the video lottery terminal, a lottery machine disguised as a video poker machine.

As discussed earlier, effective video poker strategy is based on mathematics. Using an easy-to-follow step-by-step approach, Chapter 3 explains the math behind video poker, enabling you to understand why some games—and some versions of certain games—are better than others. It also gives you a foolproof method of identifying the best-paying games in the casino, and provides invaluable strategy tables that you can use to practice the games I recommend.

As every experienced gambler knows, even when armed with perfect strategies, it's possible to lose money during a gambling session. That's why Chapter 4 provides simple and sound money management techniques that will allow your bankroll to last for your whole gambling vacation, whether it's an afternoon, a weekend, or a week. You won't want to skip this chapter, because knowing how to manage money is one of the factors that separates the winners from the losers.

Many players assume that one casino is like the next, and that it doesn't matter whether you play in a land-based commercial casino, a tribal casino, a riverboat casino, or the video poker machine at your local bar. This couldn't be further from the truth. Machines vary significantly from one venue to another, so if you want to gain the winning edge, you'll have to choose your casino with care. Chapter 5 provides a clear explanation of each type—from full-service resorts to online casinos—and steers you towards the best choices. It also looks at a range of issues you may want to consider when selecting a casino so that you can find the gambling experience that suits you best.

When visiting a casino, do you know who you're supposed to tip, and how much? Do you know if it's okay to play two machines at once, or to walk away from your machine for a short break? If not, you'll want to read Chapter 6, which offers essential rules of casino etiquette. Just as important, this chapter teaches you how to protect both yourself and your possessions while in the casino so that your gambling adventure is as safe as it is exhilarating.

Video poker can provide you with hours of fun and excitement. It is a game that you can play at your own pace, and it offers the potential of big payoffs. Most important, it rewards knowledge and smart play. It is my hope that *The Video Poker Edge* gives you the information and skills you need to not only enjoy this unique game, but—with a little luck—to go home a winner.

THE GAME
OF POKER

The exact origins of the game of poker are debated today, with most giving credit to Jonathan Green, who made the first references to "poker" in 1834. Green, who played on riverboats along the Mississippi River, called poker the "cheating game." It may have been a cheating game, but nonetheless poker was enormously popular from the start, and rapidly spread to the East Coast by way of the railroads.

Poker was a twenty-card game in the beginning; then a thirty-two-card game; and finally a game of fifty-two cards plus two Jokers. Anybody watching a movie about the Wild West is sure to see a poker game in the saloon scenes. Today it is played more than any other card game in the world, with all kinds of people competing for bragging rights.

For over a century, regardless of the number of cards used, poker was played with real cards by a group of people sitting around a table. Then in 1975, a crowd gathered around a new kind of slot machine in Las Vegas, beginning the public's fascination with video poker. At that time, the only video poker game available was Jacks or Better draw poker. Now there are over one hundred varieties of the game, and video poker is the most popular gaming option available on the casino floor.

If you're longing to get in on the fun and excitement of video poker, this chapter is the best place to start. First, I'll briefly look at the game of table poker, which is where video poker had its roots. Then, I'll introduce you to the basic game of video poker, along with some popular and commonly available variations. Finally, I'll compare the two games, so that any long-time table poker player will quickly see that video poker is by no means an electronic version of table poker, but a very different game.

TABLE POKER

There are dozens of variations of the game of table poker. For the purpose of this explanation, we'll focus on Five-Card Draw—the variation that has most in common with the game of video poker.

Table poker is played with a fifty-two-card deck. Anywhere from two to ten players can participate.

Before the cards are dealt to the individual players, the players *ante*, meaning that they place a token amount of money in the pot. Five cards are then dealt to each player. The first round of betting then occurs, with each player placing more money in the pot. If a player no longer wishes to remain in the game because he feels he has a losing hand, instead of betting, he can *fold* his hand, exiting the game and forfeiting all money he has thus far placed in the pot.

After the first betting round, each player has the option to discard one or more cards from his hand and receive new cards from the dealer. This is called the *draw.* If he prefers, however, a player may keep the hand he was originally dealt.

After the draw, there is another round of betting. Again, any player can fold and exit the game at this time.

After the second round of betting, the players show their hands, and the player with the best hand of those remaining in the game wins the pot. The winning hand is decided by hand rankings, which are described on page 7.

Sound easy? While the rules are pretty simple, when played by talented competition, the game of poker is quite challenging and involves skills in psychology and mathematics, as well as nerves of steel. For instance, a player with a poor hand may *bluff*, placing a bet as if he had a good hand with the hopes that other players will fold. Skilled players also note other players' *tells*—mannerisms that inadvertently supply information about their hands.

Before you go on to learn about video poker, it's important to look at the hand rankings used in table poker. Later in the chapter, you'll learn that while these rankings form the basis of the hand rankings used in video poker, in many cases, video poker rankings are different.

Hand Rankings in Table Poker

Anyone who even casually plays table poker has to understand poker *hand rankings*, also called the *hierarchy of hands*. In table poker, the player with the highest ranking hand wins—provided that he has not folded his hand.

If you are totally new to cards, you have to first understand that each fifty-two-card deck is composed of four *suits:* hearts, diamonds, spades, and clubs. These suits are equal in value; hearts are no more valuable than diamonds, for instance. Cards of the same suit are referred to as being "suited." For example, an Ace, King, and Ten, all in diamonds, would be a suited Ace, King, and Ten.

Within each suit are thirteen ranks. The Ace is the highest-ranking card in a suit, followed by King, Queen, Jack, Ten, Nine, Eight, Seven, Six, Five, Four, Three, and Two (or Deuce). What about the Joker? In most games of table poker, the Joker is not used. Sometimes, though, the Joker is a wild card, meaning that it can be any rank and suit that would form the highest possible hand in the hierarchy.

Hand rankings are based on probability, so that the rarer your hand, the more valuable it is. For instance, you are more likely to end up with a pair of Aces in your hand than you are to have all four Aces. For this reason, Four of a Kind is more valuable than a Pair.

Table 1.1 shows poker hand rankings from highest to lowest for table poker. Later in the chapter, you'll learn about hand rankings for video poker.

If you are not familiar with poker hand rankings, Table 1.1 on page 8 is a good place to start your education. Just be aware that every game of video poker has its own hierarchy of hands.

VIDEO POKER

While there are many variations of table poker games, there are even more versions of video poker. But before we look at some of those variations, it makes sense to present an overview of how you play the game. When reading the following discussion, please note that it presents a simplified version of how the video poker machine works. In Chapter 2, you will learn more about the mechanics of playing the game.

Name of Hand	Description	Example
Royal Flush	Ace, King, Queen, Jack, and Ten of the same suit.	
Straight Flush	Five cards of the same suit in consecutive order.	
Four of a Kind	Four cards of the same rank.	
Full House	Three cards of the same rank plus two cards of another rank.	
Flush	Any five cards of the same suit, not in consecutive order.	
Straight	Five cards of more than one suit in consecutive order.	
Three of a Kind	Three cards of the same rank.	
Two Pair	Two cards of one rank, plus two cards of another rank.	
One Pair	Two cards of the same rank.	
No Pairs	Five cards of different ranks and suits, valued only by the highest card.	

The game of video poker begins when you sit down at a video poker machine and, depending on the machine, deposit coins, bills, or a cash ticket. After you insert the money, you then press the *Max Bet* or *Bet One Credit* button, and the images of five cards appear on the screen.

Once you have seen your hand, you have the option of keeping it as is or trying to improve it by receiving replacements for one to five cards. To receive new cards, you select the cards you want to *keep*. On older machines, you hold cards by pressing the *Hold/Cancel* buttons that appear below the images of the cards. On newer machines, you can either press the *Hold/Cancel* buttons or touch the card images on the display screen. You then press the *Deal/Draw* button, and the machine displays your final hand.

When your final hand appears, the game is over. If you have a winning hand, the machine will automatically pay you according to the pay table for that game. Naturally, the better your hand, the higher the amount you'll receive.

RECOMMENDED VIDEO POKER GAMES

As mentioned earlier in the chapter, there are many different video poker games—literally hundreds—now being offered in casinos. It is beyond the scope of this book to discuss each individual game. However, below you'll find descriptions of several video poker games that are popular and widely available; that provide good returns on your money; and that are easy to play—as long as you use the strategy cards included in the back of this book. Some games are riskier than others in the short run, but I've taken care to point out the higher-risk games— Double Bonus Poker, for example—so that you can avoid them if you want to.

In the case of each game, I've guided you to the best version available. For Jacks or Better, for instance, the best game is 9/6 Jacks or Better. Be aware, though, that in a casino, you will never find a machine marked "9/6 Jacks or Better" or "8/5 Bonus Poker." Rather, you will have to examine the pay table—the table, displayed on every video poker machine, which shows you how much that game pays for each winning hand—to find what you want. Pay tables will be explained in more detail in Chapter 3, where you'll find one for each of the games recommended below. For the time being, just keep in mind that it's the

Throughout pages 10 to 16, you'll find mentions of the *expected return* (ER) of specific video poker games. What is the expected return? It is the percentage of your total bets that will theoretically be returned to you if you play that game accurately and for a long enough period of time. Cash back offers and casino promotions—which you'll learn about later in the book—can boost this percentage, and in the short run, you may win more or less than the ER. (For a complete discussion of expected returns, see page 48 of Chapter 3.)

pay table, and not the game name printed on the video poker machine, that will enable you to locate full-pay games—games that will give you the best possible return on your bet.

You are sure to find at least one of the following games in almost every casino that offers video poker. What if you enter a casino and find a game with which you are not familiar? In that case, you can press the *Help* button on the machine to find a brief description of the game. Plus, of course, the pay table will provide you with information on the winning hands. However—and this is an important caveat—you should *never* play a game without first learning the appropriate strategies and practicing their use at home. Without a clear knowledge of the game, as well as practice on tutorial software programs, your odds of losing money are high. (To learn about strategies and tutorials, see Chapter 3.)

Jacks or Better

Jacks or Better is a great game for beginners. It's easy to play correctly, its playing strategies can be applied to two other good video poker games, and—when chosen carefully—it provides good returns.

As mentioned earlier in the chapter, this was the first video poker game ever played, having been introduced in the mid-seventies by Si Redd. In fact, if you come across an older single-game machine, you will not see the name "Jacks or Better" at all, but instead will see "Draw Poker," the name used when the game was launched in 1975.

Jacks or Better uses a standard fifty-two-card deck. As the name of the game implies, the minimum rank for a winning hand is a pair of Jacks. (See the hand rankings in Table 1.2.)

I consider Jacks or Better the very best game for beginners for several reasons. First, it's easy to play correctly. Second, the playing strategies, once learned, can also be applied to two other excellent games—Bonus Poker and Bonus Poker Deluxe—both of which are discussed later in this chapter. Finally, Two Pair, a frequent hand, results in receiving double the money bet. Because this game provides such a good return for Two Pair, rather than requiring a rare hand such as Four of a Kind, it will allow you to play longer on a limited budget.

The Best Jacks or Better Game

The best version of Jacks or Better is *9/6 Jacks or Better,* which has an expected return of 99.54%. In this version of the game, you will receive 9 coins for each coin bet if you have a Full House, and 6 coins for each coin bet if you have a Flush. (See the inset on page 11 for more information on the 9/6 designation.) As explained on page 9, the machine you want will not be marked "9/6," so to find a 9/6 Jacks or Better game, you'll have to compare the pay table provided on the machine with the one I provide on page 42.

Bonus Poker Deluxe

Like Jacks or Better, this game uses a standard fifty-two-card deck and has a pair of Jacks as a minimum winning hand. It also shares the hand rankings used by Jacks or Better. (See Table 1.2.) Unlike Jacks or Better, Bonus Poker Deluxe gives you only even money for Two Pair, but if you get Four of a Kind, the game provides 80 times your bet, compensating for the poor return on Two Pair.

Because Bonus Poker Deluxe relies on Four of a Kind—an infrequent hand—to achieve a good return, you need a bigger budget to play this game, because the expected return will be achieved only with smart strategies and a sufficiently long period of play. In other words, if the game is played for only a short period of time, you may lose money. Nevertheless, I think that this game is good for beginners

What's the Difference Between a 9/6 and a 8/5 Video Poker Game?

Throughout this book, I distinguish between, say, a 9/6 Jacks or Better Game and an 8/5 Jacks or Better game. What do these designations mean? The first number in the 9/6 designation indicates that for each coin bet, you will receive 9 coins back if you have a Full House. The second number indicates that for each coin bet, you will receive 6 coins back if you have a Flush. In other words, these numbers signify the return you will receive on your money for specific hands.

Now, let's get a little into the math. If you change the 9 on the 9/6 designation to an 8, your return will be decreased by approximately 1.1%. If you change the 6 to a 5, you will lose approximately another 1.1%. All in all, you will lose about 2.2% of your return by choosing an 8/5 Jacks or Better game over a 9/6 Jacks or Better version. For a $5 wager—the cost of one maximum-bet hand on a dollar machine—this amounts to a theoretical loss of just 11 cents per hand. While this may not seem like much, if you consider the fact that a beginner will play around 600 hands per hour, the loss is about *$66 per hour of play*. That's why I always recommend full-pay games—games that give you the best return available.

because it calls for the same easy-to-use strategy employed in Jacks or Better. Therefore, if you learn to accurately play one of these two video poker games, you'll also know how to play the other. Moreover, many players find the "excitement factor" of Bonus Poker Deluxe well worth the increased risk.

The Best Bonus Poker Deluxe Game

For the best return on your money, look for *9/6 Bonus Poker Deluxe,* which will give you 9 coins for each coin bet if you have a Full House, and 6 coins for each coin bet if you have a Flush, with an expected return of 99.64%. As already explained, the machine you want will not be marked "9/6," so to find a 9/6 Bonus Poker Deluxe game, look for "Bonus Poker Deluxe" and compare the pay table on the machine with the one I provide on page 46.

Deuces Wild

The name Deuces Wild actually applies to several highly popular video poker games. Every Deuces Wild game uses a standard fifty-two-card deck. As the name suggests, all four Deuces (Twos) are wild cards, meaning that any Two can be used as a replacement for any card in order to complete a winning hand. Because you have four wild cards to help make up winning combinations, the minimum rank of a winning hand is Three of a Kind. (See the hand rankings in Table 1.3.)

In order to get the winning edge in Deuces Wild, you need to select a good game and play it accurately. Below, I discuss two excellent options.

The Best Deuces Wild Games

Full-Pay Deuces Wild is the most popular of all the many Deuces Wild games because it offers the best expected return—100.76%. This superior return is due to the fact that Four of a Kind—a frequent hand when there's four wild cards—pays more than it does in other versions of the game. The downside is that because of the good return, the casinos make the game available only in nickel and quarter denominations. Moreover, you can find this game only in states that allow casinos to offer returns over 100%. (You'll learn about state mandated paybacks in Chapter 5.)

On rare occasions, you may find $.50 or $1 versions of Full-Pay Deuces Wild. These versions generally don't last long, though, because professional and advantage recreational players monopolize the machine, preventing average (less skillful) gamblers from playing. The casino then loses money and downgrades the game to Not-So-Ugly Deuces Wild, which is still a good game, or Coyote Ugly Deuces, which is not.

This is an excellent choice for beginners because it's a *player advantage game*—a game that has an expected return of over 100%, and therefore gives an advantage to the player rather than the house. Despite this fact, it is available in many casinos, and is easy to play with the strategy card provided at the back of the book. Look for the "Deuces Wild" game name, and be sure to compare the pay table on the machine with the one on page 46 to make certain you're playing the full-pay version of the game.

Not-So-Ugly Deuces Wild is another good game with another good return—99.73%. I call this a 20/20 game because both a Full House and a Four of a Kind return 20 coins with a 5-coin bet. Not-So-Ugly Deuces Wild is offered in larger-denomination machines, and because it's legal in states that mandate less than a 100% payback, it's more widely available than Full-Pay Deuces Wild. In fact, when Full-Pay Deuces Wild is downgraded, meaning that the payback percentage is reduced, this is often the game that takes its place.

Not-So-Ugly Deuces Wild is an excellent choice for beginners—and for everyone else, as well—because with promotions, it becomes a player advantage game, and it's easy to play with the strategy card you'll find at the back of the book. Again, look for "Deuces Wild" and compare the pay table on the machine with the one on page 46 to confirm that you've found the game you want.

Bonus Poker

Bonus Poker uses a standard fifty-two-card deck and has a minimum winning hand of a pair of Jacks. (See Table 1.4 for the hand rankings.) It's called *Bonus* Poker because the payoff is greater for special Four of a Kind hands. A hand of four Twos, Threes, or Fours pays 40 times your bet, and a hand of four Aces pays 80 times your bet—both excellent payoffs. However, the return for both the Full-House and the Flush is slightly less than that in 9/6 Jacks or Better due to the extra money paid for specific Four of a Kind hands.

This is a good game for beginners because it's easy to play. In fact, the same strategies that work in Jacks or Better are also used in Bonus Poker, and many people find Bonus Poker more exciting because of the extra money paid for certain hands. This is a good game for those with a limited budget, too, because you will double your bet for Two Pair, a low-ranking and frequent hand.

It's important to understand that video poker names like Full-Pay Deuces Wild and Not-So-Ugly Deuces Wild were given to the games by players—not by video poker machine manufacturers or casinos. Throughout this book, I have used these descriptive names for ease of reference, but when you go to a casino, don't expect to find them on the machines. Instead, you'll have to look for the casino name—Deuces Wild, in both these cases—and compare pay tables to find the game you want. (For more information on game names, see the inset on page 58 of Chapter 3.)

The Best Bonus Poker Game

For the best return on your money, look for *8/5 Bonus Poker,* which will return 8 coins for each coin bet if you have a Full House, and 5 coins for each coin bet if you have a Flush. While this may not sound great once you've read about 9/6 games, it's a far better alternative than your other option—7/4 Bonus Poker—and provides a 99.17% expected return.

As already explained, the machine you want will not be marked "8/5," so to find a 8/5 Bonus Poker game, you'll have to look for "Bonus Poker" and compare the pay table on the machine with the one on page 45.

Double Bonus Poker

Like Bonus Poker, this game uses a standard fifty-two-card deck, and the minimum winning hand is a pair of Jacks. The two games also share the same hand ranking table. (See Table. 1.4.) However, unlike Bonus Poker, Double Bonus poker pays only even money for Two Pair. (In other words, you get back the same amount you wagered.) On the other hand, as the name implies, it awards double the amount wagered for the special Four of a Kind hands mentioned in Bonus Poker. That is, it pays 80 times your bet for four Twos, four Threes, or four Fours; and 160 times your bet for four Aces.

Again, many find this game exciting because of the big payout for certain Four of a Kind hands. Just keep in mind that like any game that relies on infrequent hands to achieve a good return, Double Bonus Poker can be expensive in the short run, and requires a relatively big budget. Nevertheless, I think this is a great game even for beginners. It provides a good return when you select the version recommended below, and it can be played close to perfect with the strategy card included in the back of this book. Moreover, the game is available in many casinos.

The Best Double Bonus Poker Game

For the best return on your money, look for *10/7 Double Bonus Poker,* which will give you 10 coins for each coin bet if you have a Full House, and 7 coins for each coin bet if you have a Flush. The expected return on this game is excellent—100.17%.

As already explained, machines are never marked "10/7," so to find the game you want, you'll have to look for "Double Bonus Poker" and match up the pay table on the machine with the one on page 47.

Double Double Bonus Poker

This game uses a standard fifty-two-card deck, and the minimum winning hand is a pair of Jacks. (See Table 1.6 for the hand rankings.) Like Double Bonus Poker, you win only even money for Two Pair, a frequent combination. And you win less for a Straight, a Flush, and a Full House than you do in Double Bonus Poker. To compensate for the lower return for frequent winning hands, though, Double Double Bonus Poker pays a high return for specific rare hand combinations.

This game introduces a new concept, a card called a *kicker*. In Double Double Bonus Poker, a kicker is an Ace, Two, Three, or Four, and here's how it works: If you have a special Four of a Kind plus a kicker, you win double the amount paid in Double Bonus. This means that if you have four Twos, Threes, or Fours, and the fifth card is an Ace, Two, Three, or Four, you win 160 times your bet, instead of 80 times your bet. If you have four Aces and the fifth card is a Two, Three, or Four, you win 400 times your bet, more than doubling the payoff in Double Bonus Poker.

Like several of the games already discussed, this one demands a higher budget because frequent hand combinations have relatively poor payoffs, while the best payoffs are for relatively rare hands. Therefore, you may endure a bumpy ride before you see a good return. But if you choose the "best game" option described below, you can do well even if you're a beginner. Moreover, the game is easy and fun to play, and provides a real adrenaline rush when you draw a rare high-paying hand.

The Best Double Double Bonus Poker Game

For the best return on your money, look for *9/6 Double Double Bonus Poker* and search for a progressive jackpot, which provides bigger payoffs for special Four of a Kind and Royal Flush hands. (You'll learn

If you enjoy the excitement of Double Double Bonus Poker, but your small budget makes you shy away from a high-risk game, consider playing at a lower-denomination machine—at a quarter instead of a dollar machine, for instance. This may allow you to keep playing until you hit a high-paying hand combination. (For more tips on money management, see Chapter 4.)

Sometimes you can find a 10/6 or even a 10/7 version of Double Double Bonus Poker. If you spot one, grab a seat and play, because payoffs like this are rare.

about progressive jackpots in Chapter 4.) Even if you don't find a progressive jackpot, the expected return on a 9/6 Double Double Bonus Poker Game is 98.98%.

The machine you want will not, of course, be marked "9/6," so you'll have to first locate a game marked "Double Double Bonus Poker," and then match up the pay table on the machine with the one on page 45.

Pick'Em Poker

Often, casinos include Pick 'Em Poker in special promotions, making this game a great choice.

This game uses a standard fifty-two-card deck, and the minimum winning hand is a pair of Nines. (See Table 1.5.) While this isn't unusual, the game itself is very different from the ones I've just discussed.

In Pick 'Em Poker, the game starts when the computer deals two exposed cards on the left side of the video display screen, and two stacks of three cards each on the right side of the screen, with only the top card of each stack exposed. (Note that you won't see an actual "stack"; you'll just see the exposed card.) You must hold the two exposed cards on the left, but you do get to choose which of the two stacks on the right you want to hold. Once you make your decision, the computer will expose the two hidden cards in the chosen stack, and you will have your final hand.

Note that because Pick 'Em Poker does not allow you to replace any unwanted cards on the left side of the screen, the game diminishes your chance of achieving a high hand after the draw. That's why you are paid for a relatively low-ranking hand—a pair of Nines.

Because you are paid for a statistically frequent hand, this is a good choice for people on a limited budget. It is also a good game for beginners because the strategies are easy to learn and use. Moreover, because the payback percentage is less than 100%, Pick 'Em Poker can be found in a large number of casinos.

The Best Pick 'Em Poker Game

For the best return on your money, you'll want *Full-Pay Pick 'Em Poker*, which will give you an expected return of 99.95%. Just look for "Pick 'Em Poker"—it won't say "Full-Pay"—and compare the pay table on the machine with the one on page 47 to find the version you want.

Hand Rankings in Video Poker

On page 8, you learned the hand rankings for table poker. Below, you will find hand ranking tables for all of the video poker games recommended in the previous pages. You'll soon see that while the hand rankings for video poker are based on those of table poker, there are differences, not only because of the special rules that govern each video poker game—think of Jacks or Better and its minimum winning hand of two Jacks—but also because of the wild cards used in many games.

As you've already learned, due to the advantage provided by wild cards in games such as Deuces Wild, the minimum winning hand in these games is of a higher rank than the minimum winning hand in non-wild card games. Note, too, that a *natural hand*—a hand that does not use wild cards—sometimes ranks higher than a corresponding hand that contains wild cards. For instance, a natural Royal Flush will pay more than a Wild Royal Flush.

Although this has been explained earlier in the chapter, I can't overemphasize the fact that most games—Jacks or Better, Deuces Wild, Bonus Poker, and more—have several versions, each of which may have different hand rankings as well as different payouts for different hands *even though the names printed on the machines may be the same for the various games.* For this reason, you must check pay tables—comparing the one on the machine to those presented on pages 45 to 47—before you choose to play a video poker game. This is the only way you'll be able to identify high-paying machines.

Finally, it's important to understand that although table poker players usually physically move their cards around to put them in some type of order, in video poker, the cards can appear on the screen in *any* order. For instance, you may draw a Royal Flush in which the cards, from left to right, read Ten, King, Ace, Queen, and Jack, and you will not be able to move these cards around. That is why it is so important to maintain your focus after the cards are dealt so that you will be sure to recognize a winning hand—or a potential winning hand—when it appears. (The pay table will highlight winning combinations when they appear, but will not highlight good hands that could *become* winning hands with smart play.) In the following video poker hand ranking tables, the cards *do* appear in consecutive order so that you can more easily see and understand each combination. This will almost never

A *natural hand* is a winning hand that contains no wild cards. In some video poker games, this hand ranks higher than a corresponding hand that includes wild cards.

Table 1.2. Video Poker Hand Rankings From Highest to Lowest for Jacks or Better and Bonus Poker Deluxe

Name of Hand	Description	Example
Royal Flush	Ace, King, Queen, Jack, and Ten of the same suit.	AS, KS, QS, JS, 10S
Straight Flush*	Five cards of the same suit in consecutive order.	JH, 10H, 9H, 8H, 7H
Four of a Kind*	Four cards of the same rank.	6C, 6H, 6S, 6D, KC
Full House	Three cards of the same rank plus two cards of another rank.	3D, 3C, 3H, QS, QH
Flush	Five cards of the same suit, not in consecutive order.	AD, JD, 9D, 7D, 3D
Straight	Five cards of more than one suit in consecutive order.	9D, 8H, 7C, 6C, 5H
Three of a Kind	Three cards of the same rank.	7D, 7C, 7H, JD, 3C
Two Pair	Two cards of one rank, plus two cards of another rank.	KH, KC, 6D, 6S, 10D
Jacks or Better	Two cards of the same rank, with the minimum paying hand being a pair of Jacks.	JD, JS, QS, 8H, 4C

*Note that these are the rankings as you will see them on the ranking portion of the pay tables of both Jacks or Better and Bonus Poker Deluxe. In Bonus Poker Deluxe, however, Four of a Kind will pay more than a Straight Flush.

Table 1.3. Video Poker Hand Rankings From Highest to Lowest for Full-Pay Deuces Wild and Not-So-Ugly Deuces Wild*

Name of Hand	Description	Example
Royal Flush	Ace, King, Queen, Jack, and Ten of the same suit achieved without Deuces (Twos).	AS, KS, QS, JS, 10S
Four Deuces	Four Deuces (Twos).	2H, 2S, 2D, 2C, 10D
Wild Royal Flush	A Royal Flush achieved with one or more Deuces (Twos).	AD, KD, 2S, 2H, 10D
Five of a Kind	Five cards of the same rank achieved with one or more Deuces (Twos).	8H, 8C, 8S, 2S, 2D
Straight Flush	Five cards of the same suit in consecutive order achieved with or without Deuces (Twos).	JH, 10H, 2S, 8H, 7H
Four of a Kind	Four cards of the same rank achieved with or without Deuces (Twos).	8H, 8C, 2D, 2S, 5H
Full House	Three cards of the same rank plus two cards of another rank, achieved with or without Deuces (Twos).	JH, JS, 2D, 8S, 8H
Flush	Five cards of the same suit, not in consecutive order, achieved with or without Deuces (Twos).	KD, JD, 8D, 5D, 2S,
Straight	Five cards of more than one suit in consecutive order achieved with or without Deuces (Twos).	KD, 2H, JH, 10D, 9S
Three of a Kind	Three cards of the same rank achieved with or without Deuces (Twos).	8C, 2D, 8H, 7S, 5D

*Note that the rankings in this table also apply to Loose Deuces, Illinois/Airport Deuces, Colorado Deuces, Sam's Town Deuces, Downtown Deuces, and several Coyote Ugly versions of Deuces Wild. (The pay schedule for each of these games is different, however.) Different rankings are used for Deluxe Deuces, Bonus Deuces, Barbaric Deuces, and Super Bonus Deuces.

Table 1.4. **Video Poker Hand Rankings From Highest to Lowest for Bonus Poker and Double Bonus Poker**

Name of Hand	Description	Example
Royal Flush	Ace, King, Queen, Jack, and Ten of the same suit.	AS, KS, QS, JS, 10S
Straight Flush*	Five cards of the same suit in consecutive order.	JH, 10H, 9H, 8H, 7H
Four Aces*	Four Aces.	AH, AD, AS, AC, 9S
Four Twos, Threes, or Fours*	Four Twos, Threes, or Fours.	4H, 4D, 4S, 4C, 8H
Four Fives to Kings	Four Fives, Sixes, Sevens, Eights, Nines, Tens, Jacks, Queens, or Kings.	KH, KD, KS, KC, 5C
Full House	Three cards of the same rank plus two cards of another rank.	8H, 8C, 8S, 9S, 9C
Flush	Five cards of the same suit, not in consecutive order.	AH, JH, 7H, 5H, 2H
Straight	Five cards of more than one suit in consecutive order.	JC, 10C, 9D, 8H, 7S
Three of a Kind	Three cards of the same rank.	8H, 8S, 8C, 9D, 6S
Two Pair	Two cards of one rank, plus two cards of another rank.	JH, JS, 5D, 5H, 4S
Jacks or Better	Two cards of the same rank, with the minimum paying hand being a pair of Jacks.	QH, QC, 7D, 6H, 2C

*Note that these are the rankings as you will see them on the ranking portion of the pay table. However, the Straight Flush will pay less than Four Aces, Twos, Threes, or Fours in Double Bonus Poker, and less than Four Aces in Bonus Poker.

Table 1.5. **Video Poker Hand Rankings From Highest to Lowest for Pick 'Em Poker**

Name of Hand	Description	Example
Royal Flush	Ace, King, Queen, Jack, and Ten of the same suit.	AS, KS, QS, JS, 10S
Straight Flush	Five cards of the same suit in consecutive order.	JH, 10H, 9H, 8H, 7H
Four of a Kind	Four cards of the same rank.	9D, 9S, 9H, 9C, 10D
Full House	Three cards of the same rank plus two cards of another rank.	8H, 8C, 8S, 9S, 9C
Flush	Five cards of the same suit, not in consecutive order.	AH, JH, 7H, 5H, 2H,
Straight	Five cards of more than one suit in consecutive order.	JD, 10C, 9D, 8H, 7S
Three of a Kind	Three cards of the same rank.	8H, 8S, 8C, 6D, 5S
Two Pair	Two cards of one rank, plus two cards of another rank.	JH, JS, 5D, 5H, 4S
Nines or Better	Two cards of the same rank, with the minimum paying hand being a pair of Nines.	9H, 9C, 7D, 6H, 2C

Table 1.6. **Video Poker Hand Rankings From Highest to Lowest
for Double Double Bonus Poker**

Name of Hand	Description	Example
Royal Flush	Ace, King, Queen, Jack, and Ten of the same suit.	AS, KS, QS, JS, 10S
Straight Flush*	Five cards of the same suit in consecutive order.	JH, 10H, 9H, 8H, 7H
Four Aces with a Two, Three, or Four*†	Four Aces with a Two, Three, or Four.	AH, AD, AS, AC, 4H
Four Twos, Threes, or Fours with an Ace, Two, Three, or Four*†	Four Twos, Threes, or Fours with an Ace, Two, Three, or Four.	4H, 4D, 4S, 4C, AS
Four Aces*†	Four Aces.	AH, AD, AS, AC, 6S
Four Twos, Threes, or Fours*	Four Twos, Threes, or Fours.	4H, 4D, 4S, 4C, 8H
Four Fives to Kings	Four Fives, Sixes, Seven, Eights, Nines, Tens, Jacks, Queens, or Kings.	KH, KD, KS, KC, 5C
Full House	Three cards of the same rank plus two cards of another rank.	8H, 8C, 8S, 9S, 9C
Flush	Five cards of the same suit, not in consecutive order.	AH, JH, 7H, 5H, 2H
Straight	Five cards of more than one suit in consecutive order.	JD, 10C, 9D, 8H, 7S
Three of a Kind	Three cards of the same rank.	8H, 8S, 8C, 6D, 5S
Two Pair	Two cards of one rank, plus two cards of another rank.	JH, JS, 5D, 5H, 4S
Jacks or Better	Two cards of the same rank, with the minimum paying hand being a pair of Jacks.	QH, QC, 7D, 6H, 2C

*Note that these are the rankings as you will see them on the ranking portion of the pay table. However, the Straight Flush will pay less than Four Aces, Twos, Threes, or Fours either with or without a kicker. Four Fives through Kings will pay the same as a Straight Flush.
† Note that Aces, Twos, Threes, and Fours are called "kickers" in this game.

happen on your video poker screen. The good news is that if by chance a video poker Royal Flush appears in ascending or descending order, you will have a *Sequential Royal,* which in some games pays more than a Royal Flush whose cards are in random order.

UNDERSTANDING THE DIFFERENCES
BETWEEN VIDEO POKER AND TABLE POKER

If you're a table poker player and are about to play video poker for the first time, it's important to be aware of the many ways in which the games differ from each other. Anyone who persists in thinking of video poker as an electronic version of table poker, and makes strategy decisions with that in mind, is in for an unpleasant surprise. On the other hand, the player who recognizes the unique nature of video poker is well on his way to understanding successful video poker strategy. The following are the most important differences between the two games.

> Don't make the mistake of playing video poker as if it were an electronic version of table poker. Video poker is a unique game that requires its own special strategies.

❏ In table poker, your hand has to beat the hands held by the other players remaining in the game. In video poker, your hand has to match a winning combination listed on the pay table. You are the only player, and the video poker machine itself, of course, is not trying to beat your hand.

❏ In table poker, you can improve your success rate by using psychological strategies such as bluffing. Because video poker is played on a machine, psychological strategies will not work.

❏ All table poker games involve several rounds of betting. In video poker, in the vast majority of cases, you "bet" only once—when you insert coins in the machine at the start of the game or press a button indicating the size of your bet.

❏ In table poker, there is always a winner. This means that you can win the pot without holding even a pair as long as your hand is better than the hands of the other players remaining in the game. In video poker, you will not win if your hand does not match a hand listed on the pay table.

❏ In table poker, in most cases, it doesn't matter if you win with a low hand or a high hand. A win is a win, and a Royal Flush entitles you to no more money than a Pair. In video poker, the higher the hand on the hierarchy table, the more money you win.

❏ In table poker, if two players hold the same winning combination— a Full House, for instance—the specific cards in each hand can determine the winner of the game. For example, if two players both have a Full House, the person with the highest Three of a Kind portion of the Full House wins. In video poker, in most cases, you are paid the amount indicated on the pay table for each winning combination. All Full Houses pay the same, for instance, unless the pay table says otherwise.

❏ In table poker, to clarify a hand both for himself and for the dealer, a player places the cards in his hand in sequential order or otherwise organizes them into winning combinations. In video poker, this is not possible, since the cards can't be physically moved.

❏ In video poker, a player can get a *Sequential Royal,* which is a Royal Flush in which the cards appear on the screen in either ascending (10, J, Q, K, A) or descending (A, K,Q, J, 10) order. Because this is a very rare occurrence, some video poker games offer additional large jackpots for Sequential Royals. In table poker, a Sequential Royal has no meaning, since a player almost always physically moves the cards around in his hand, placing them in consecutive order.

By now, you probably have a fairly good idea of how video poker is played, as well as familiarity with some of the best video poker games. But there's a big difference between gaining theoretical knowledge of a casino game and actually sitting down at a machine and playing it—especially if you've never seen a video poker machine before. Where will you find the pay table for each machine? What button should you press to start the game? What should you do if you accidentally hold the wrong cards? That's what Chapter 2 is all about.

GETTING TO KNOW YOUR VIDEO POKER MACHINE

It isn't difficult to use a video poker machine. In fact, casinos make these machines as easy to use as possible so that new players won't hesitate to sit down and try their luck. But if you want to feel comfortable the first time you sit down and play video poker, and, more important, if you want to avoid some very expensive and aggravating mistakes, you'll find it worthwhile to get to know the standard video poker machine.

If you've never seen a video poker machine before, keep in mind that this machine is similar in appearance to a modern slot machine. In fact, some machines contain both video poker and slot choices on their multi-game menus. But because video poker allows you to make decisions, the playing process is more complex and involves the use of more controls than you would need if you were playing slots.

This chapter first introduces you to the outside of the video poker machine—to the components that provide you with important information about your chosen game, allow you to affect the outcome of the game, and enable you to earn valuable comps (complimentary services). It then introduces you to the random number generator, which is the all-important internal component that allows savvy players to gain the winning edge through proven strategies. Finally, the chapter debunks some common video poker myths that can prevent you from making the best playing decisions possible, and steers you away from video lottery terminals—lottery machines that masquerade as video poker machines.

THE OUTSIDE OF THE VIDEO POKER MACHINE

Where do you put cash in a video poker machine? Where do you find the pay table? What buttons do you use to hold some cards and discard others? What should you do if you mistakenly hold the *wrong* cards?

If you're new to the game of video poker, these are important questions. Even if you're not new to the game, there may be some "widgets" that you find puzzling. By learning the function of each control, you will take one more step toward gaining that winning edge.

The Candle

On top of each video poker machine is a cylindrical light, a portion of which is color-coded to show the denomination of currency you can bet at that machine. On most machines, the candle is white on top. Below that, a red light indicates nickels; a yellow light, quarters; a blue light, dollars; and a purple light, higher denominations. On multi-denomination machines, the color below the white portion of the candle usually represents the highest denomination allowed.

The candle is used to indicate other things, as well. By pushing the *Change/Call Attendant* button, you will light the top of the candle and thus let the casino staff know that you need service. On older machines, the candle flashes when the coin hopper inside the machine is empty. On newer machines, the candle flashes when the machine is out of the paper used to print cash tickets; when there is a malfunction; and when you win a *hand-paid jackpot*—a jackpot that the casino chooses to deliver by hand.

> Although each casino decides the amount that requires a jackpot to be hand-paid, in most cases, a win over $500 will result in a hand-delivered jackpot.

The Manufacturer's Glass

On the front of every single-game machine—also called a dedicated or stand-alone machine—above the display screen, a piece of glass is emblazoned with the name of the game you can play on that machine, such as Draw Poker (Jacks or Better) or Deuces Wild. On older machines,

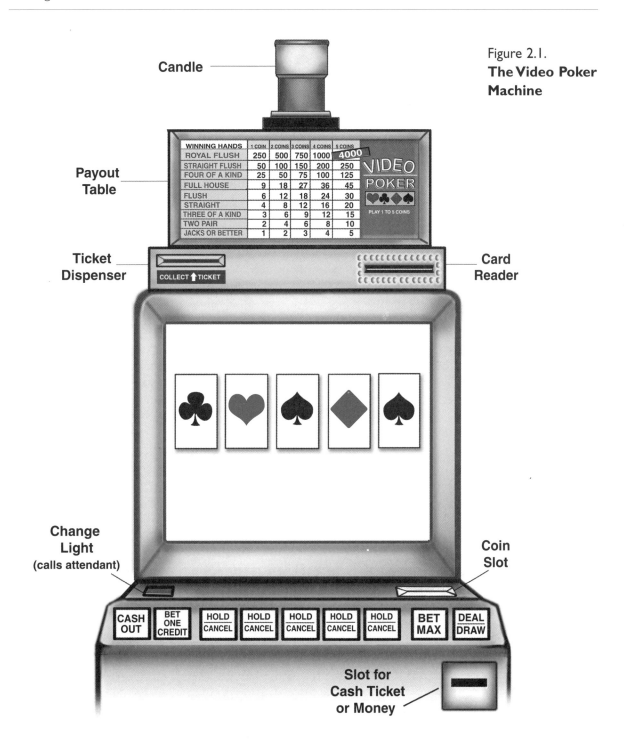

Candle

Payout
Table

WINNING HANDS	1 COIN	2 COINS	3 COINS	4 COINS	5 COINS
ROYAL FLUSH	250	500	750	1000	4000
STRAIGHT FLUSH	50	100	150	200	250
FOUR OF A KIND	25	50	75	100	125
FULL HOUSE	9	18	27	36	45
FLUSH	6	12	18	24	30
STRAIGHT	4	8	12	16	20
THREE OF A KIND	3	6	9	12	15
TWO PAIR	2	4	6	8	10
JACKS OR BETTER	1	2	3	4	5

Figure 2.1.
**The Video Poker
Machine**

VIDEO
POKER

PLAY 1 TO 5 COINS

Ticket
Dispenser

COLLECT ↑ TICKET

Card
Reader

Change
Light
(calls attendant)

Coin
Slot

CASH
OUT

BET
ONE
CREDIT

HOLD
CANCEL

HOLD
CANCEL

HOLD
CANCEL

HOLD
CANCEL

HOLD
CANCEL

BET
MAX

DEAL
DRAW

Slot for
Cash Ticket
or Money

the pay table for that game is also sometimes displayed on the glass. On newer multi-game machines, the machine displays the brand—usually Game King or Game Maker. On these machines, there is not enough room to list all of the games offered, much less their pay tables.

The Video Display Screen

Every video poker machine has a display screen on which the cards appear, along with other information. The placement of this screen varies according to the machine, which comes in two basic models. In the upright model, the video display screen faces the player, much like the screen of a computer. In the table-top model, the screen is on the top of the machine, parallel to the floor.

As already mentioned, video poker machines differ not only in the location of their display screen, but also in the number of games they offer. While some machines offer just one video poker game, others offer several. The number of games presented affects the information that appears on the screen.

The Single-Game Display Screen

When the video poker machine offers only one game, the pay table for that game is displayed on the screen when you first walk up to the machine. As you will learn in Chapter 3, the pay table shows not only the hand rankings for that game, but also the number of coins won for each winning hand, based on the number of coins bet. If the game is tied into a progressive jackpot, the pay table also shows the amount of that jackpot. (See pages 63 to 67 in Chapter 3 for a discussion of progressive jackpots.)

The Multi-Game Display Screen

If the video poker machine offers either several different games or several denominations of the same game, the screen will not display the pay table when you first walk up to the machine. Instead, it will offer a menu of denominations and games from which to choose. You will first select the denomination you want to play—quarters, dollars, or another denomination being offered. You will then select the game and carefully examine the pay table to make sure that you have chosen the game you

Don't deposit your money in the video poker machine until you have examined the pay table for the game you selected. As you learned in Chapter 1, two games can have the same name but very different payoffs. The pay table will tell you whether you're getting the game you want.

want. This is necessary because the choice of a specific denomination sometimes changes the pay table.

On both single- and multi-game machines, the video screen will display other information as well. In the lower right-hand side of the screen, the machine will register the amount of your credits as you insert money or tokens. As you play, the screen will reflect your changing credit by diminishing the amount when you lose, and increasing the amount when you win. This will enable you to keep track of your changing bankroll.

Once the cards have been dealt at the beginning of a game, if you have a winning combination, both the combination and the amount of coins won will be highlighted on the screen. In most machines, the pay table is either dark blue or black and the column corresponding to the number of coins you bet is bright red. Winning combinations are further highlighted in either white or yellow on the horizontal hand ranking line.

When you hold a card, the word "HOLD" will appear above or below the appropriate card. When you receive your final hand, "GAME OVER" will appear on the display screen, usually in the center or to the right.

The Buttons

Once you have determined the game you are going to play, you will deposit either money or a cash ticket in the coin slot or bill validator. (You'll learn more about this on page 31.) You will then use the various buttons to play your game of choice. The following discussions examine those buttons in the order in which they are used.

The Bet One Credit and Bet Max Buttons

After you deposit your money, to begin playing, you will choose one of two buttons, the *Bet One Credit* button or the *Bet Max* button.

The *Bet One Credit* button is located below the display screen, and is the second button from the left on most machines. You must press this button once for each coin you want to bet. You can bet from one coin to maximum coins using this button. You then must press the *Deal/Draw* button to see your cards. (You'll learn more about the *Deal/Draw* button later in the chapter.)

The names of various buttons, as well as those of other video poker machine features, differ from machine to machine. New machines are constantly being produced with slightly different control names. So don't be confused if some of the terms used on your machine are a little different from the ones I provide in this book. Whether a button is labeled *Change* or *Change/ Call Attendant*, for instance, the button will have the same function and the same location on the machine.

The *Bet Max* button should be used *only* when you're betting maximum coins. Make sure you know the maximum number of coins for that particular game before pressing the button, because once the button is depressed, it will be too late to decrease your bet.

If you choose to play the maximum number of coins, the wisest choice is to simply press the *Bet Max* button—sometimes called the *Play 5 Credits* or *Play Max Credits* button—which is usually located second from the right on the machine. Most machines have a maximum bet of 5 coins, but a few nickel and quarter machines have 10-coin max bets and some machines even have 20-coin max bets, so it's important to check the pay table before pressing *Bet Max*. After you press the button, the cards will be dealt and their images will appear on the display screen. (There will be no need to press the *Deal/Draw* button.) Just be aware that once you've pressed either the *Bet One Credit* or *Bet Max* button, it will be too late to change your mind and decrease your bet.

The Hold/Cancel Buttons

As described earlier in the chapter, once your cards are dealt, if you have a winning combination, both the combination and the amount of coins won will be highlighted on the pay table displayed on your screen. If you are a beginner, be sure to check the pay table so that you don't accidentally throw away a high-ranking winner.

If you do not have a winning hand, or if you have a low-ranking winning hand but see the potential to draw a higher hand, you can choose to hold certain cards and get replacements for others by using the *Hold/Cancel* buttons. These buttons are located below the display screen, with one button beneath each of the five cards. Note that use of a *Hold/Cancel* button causes the machine to *hold* that card. If you want to discard a card, you simply refrain from pushing the button below it. If you are playing a touch screen machine, you have the choice of using the *Hold/Cancel* buttons as just described or of touching the cards on the display screen. If you change your mind, you can either touch the screen a second time or press the *Hold/Cancel* button a second time. Once you have made your decision, check the display screen to make sure that the word "HELD" appears either below or above each card that you want to keep.

The Deal/Draw Button

As you learned on page 27, the *Deal/Draw* button is sometimes used to get the first hand of cards. This button, which is found below the display screen, must also be pressed once you have chosen the cards you want to hold. At that point, your final hand will be shown on the screen. If you have drawn a winning hand, both the winning combination and the amount won will be highlighted on the pay table located on the display screen. Usually, the words "GAME OVER" will appear on the screen, as well.

If you want to play another game and bet the same amount wagered on the first game, you can simply press the *Deal/Draw* button once more, and your new hand will appear. If you want to change the amount of your bet, you should press either the *Bet Max* button or the *Bet One Credit* button.

The Cash Out Button

When you no longer wish to play, press the *Cash Out* button, which is usually the first button on the left below the display screen. On older machines, the coins will then be dispensed and fall into the tray located beneath the display screen. On the newer TITO (ticket-in ticket-out) machines, a cash ticket sometimes called a *quicket* will be dispensed by the machine. Some touch screen machines require you to touch the "CASH OUT" message that appears on the display screen after you press the *Cash Out* button.

Sometimes a "CALL ATTENDANT" message appears on the machine at this point. This can mean that the machine has run out of paper, or that you are cashing out more than the amount predetermined by the casino. If the former, a mechanic will come and fill the ticket dispenser. If the latter, the candle on your machine will flash to signal an attendant, who will pay you the amount by hand, as described on page 24.

The Change/Call Attendant Button

The *Change/Call Attendant* button—which on newer machines is simply labeled *Change*—is located on the left side of the machine, usually below the display screen and directly above the *Bet One Credit* button. Often this button is red for easy identification. When pressed, the light on the upper portion of the candle flashes, signaling that you need help. Use this button if you need change, if you need a mechanic, if you want cocktail service, or if you desire any other type of assistance.

When playing your first hand on a video poker machine, be sure to use the *Bet One Credit* or *Bet Max* button to determine the size of your bet. If you press the *Deal/Draw* button, you will automatically repeat the bet made by the last person who played on that machine.

The Touch Screen Buttons

So far, I have for the most part offered information on the physical buttons found on video poker machines. But, as mentioned earlier, newer machines have touch screens, and these screens have "buttons" that are located below the images of the cards. The placement of these buttons varies somewhat from machine to machine, but the function of each of them is fairly standard.

Multi-Hand Video Poker Machines

Most of the video poker games played in casinos are single-hand games. You play only one virtual hand of cards at a time. But if you desire, another option is available—an option that is a huge draw to many players.

In 2000, Ernie Moody introduced *multi-hand machines*—video poker machines that allow you to play from one to a hundred hands of the same game at the same time. Even though all hands are part of the same game, a separate deck of cards is used for every hand.

Multi-hand machines, which are also called *multi-play* and *multi-line machines,* have a touch screen and require either bills or a cash ticket.

For the most part, the touch screens on these machines offer the same buttons found on regular video poker machines. Once you select both the game and the denomination, you will see the final hands from the previous game, with the main hand at the bottom of the screen and the other hands above the main hand. The pay table for the chosen game will appear in the margin of the screen, with the highest ranking hands on the left and the lowest on the right.

At that point, you can decide how many hands you want to play by pressing or touching the appropriate *Bet* button. The hands will then appear—again, with the main hand at the bottom of the screen and the other hands above. Note that the cards in all of the hands will be identical. Moreover, once you choose the cards you want to hold in the main hand, the exact same cards will be held in all the other hands. But because a separate virtual deck of fifty-two cards is used for each hand you play, the final hands you receive on the draw will all be different. Once you receive your final hands, the machine will automatically total your credits according to the game's pay table.

Multi-hand machines are widely available and, as mentioned earlier, are popular with many players. Why? If you are lucky enough to be dealt a *pat hand*—a winning combination that allows you to hold all five cards as dealt—you will be paid for every one of the separate hands! But these games are also very risky. You may tell yourself that you're playing for pennies, but if you choose a 100-play Bet Max, the "penny" machine will cost you $5 per hand. So choose multi-hand games only if you are familiar with the strategies for that game, if the pay table is good, and if your budget allows you to "multiply" your gambling risk.

When you touch the *More Games* button, a menu of games will be displayed on the screen. You can then touch the game you wish to play as well as the denomination, if more than one is offered. At that point, the pay table for the chosen game will appear on the screen, and, below it, the cards from the last hand played. If you want to see only the pay table, touch the *See Pays* button. This pay table will have *Bet Up* and *Bet Down* buttons that will allow you to highlight the appropriate column for the number of coins you wish to bet. Once you've decided on the game and your wager, you can touch the *Return to Game* button and begin to play.

If you find a game that is unfamiliar to you but that piques your interest, simply touch the *Help* button, and the machine will briefly explain the rules of the game. Once you have read the information, the *Return to Game* button will give you access to the previous display screen.

When playing your video poker game of choice, you will be able to use either the physical buttons located below the display screen or the touch screen buttons to select the cards you want to hold. If you have been playing for a while and want the cards to be dealt either faster or slower, you can easily modify the speed of play by using the *Speed* button located on the left of the touch screen. When you draw a winning hand, some machines will allow you to play for double or nothing by pressing the *Double Down* button, which is found on the right of the touch screen.

If the graphics on the video display screen are unclear, or you would like the sounds made by the machine to be louder or softer, simply push the *Change* button. You will then be able to ask for a mechanic who can make the necessary adjustments. If you are using an older machine that doesn't have a *Speed* button, a mechanic can even make the machine deal your cards faster or slower.

Coin Slots, Bill Acceptors, and Ticket Acceptors

In older video poker machines, you deposit coins in the coin slot, or you place bills in the bill validator. Denominations range from pennies to $500, and older machines accept both coins and bills—although most players deposit bills. As mentioned earlier, once your money is accepted, the machine will register the amount of your credit on the lower right-hand side of the video screen. The machine will automatically convert the money deposited to the proper number of credits, based on the denomination you choose to play. As you play, the screen will reflect your changing credit.

More and more, TITO machines are becoming the only machines available in casinos. These machines have a slot that accepts either a

After each playing session, be sure to total all of your cash tickets before handing them to the cashier. This is done by inserting them, one after the other, in the bill validator of any slot or video poker machine. The machine will then print out one cash ticket—a total of all your cash tickets—that you can take to the cashier. This will speed the redemption process and is considered a courtesy to the cashier and the other players.

cash ticket or paper currency. Just like coin-slot machines, TITO machines register your credit on the screen so that you can keep an eye on your bankroll.

As explained earlier in the chapter, at the end of play, you must hit the *Cash Out* button. If you have any remaining credit, coins will spill out of an older-style machine. A TITO machine, though, will dispense a bar-coded ticket through a slot labeled "COLLECT TICKET," located above and to the left of the display screen. This ticket can be exchanged for cash by the casino cashiers or at a self-redemption machine. If you fail to remove your ticket, the machine will beep repeatedly.

The Card Reader Slot

Above the display screen and usually on the right of the machine, you'll find a *Card Reader Slot*,—which may be labeled "Card Reader Slot," "Insert Card Here," "Slot Card," or "Card Reader." When you properly insert your slot club card, a rectangular message screen located parallel to the slot on the center of the machine will tell you when the card is properly inserted by greeting you by name. When the card is improperly inserted, an error message will appear instead. If you continue to get a "REINSERT CARD" message, press the *Change/Call Attendant* button and somebody will help you. Most machines have small lights around the slot that flash yellow when there is no card inserted, green when the card is properly inserted, and red if the card is inserted incorrectly. (You'll learn more about slot club cards on page 33 of this chapter and on page 91 of Chapter 4.)

THE RANDOM NUMBER GENERATOR

Avoid the common mistake of leaving your cash ticket on the windshield of your car with the intention of using it the next day. When exposed to the sun, these tickets quickly turn black.

You now know about the visible portions of the video poker machine. But just as important as the display screen, buttons, and lights is the internal component of the machine that makes video poker a game of skill rather than a variation of the slot machine. This component is called a random number generator (RNG). Is it possible to win at video poker without understanding the RNG? Sure it is. But because all of the strategies presented in this book are based on the randomness of the cards being dealt, and because so many myths exist regarding the way the RNG deals both the original hand and the draw, the RNG merits some discussion.

Debunking Video Poker Myths

Whether you're a seasoned video poker player or someone who's never stepped foot inside a casino, you may have heard a myth or two about the game. Some myths are certainly intriguing, but if you base your strategies on these misconceptions, you're likely to make bad playing decisions. Below, I've presented some common video poker myths along with the facts.

Myth: Video poker machines are programmed to run in winning and losing cycles, so every "cold" streak of bad hands is followed by a "hot" streak of winning hands.
A video poker machine is not programmed to have "hot" or "cold" streaks. The machine's random number generator (RNG) uses an algorithm to determine the cards you will receive on both the deal and the draw. Because the dealing of cards is random—meaning that there are no discernible patterns—it's impossible to predict whether a machine will win or lose based on past hands. (See page 32 to learn more about the random number generator.)

Myth: After discarding cards, you will sometimes receive the same cards on the draw.
This is completely false. Once you decide to throw a card away by not pushing the *Hold/Cancel* button, that card will be out of play for the rest of that game. You may receive a card of the same rank—if you discard the Eight of Hearts, for instance, you may receive the Eight of Diamonds—but you will not receive the exact same card you discarded.

Myth: The machine will pay either more or less if you use a casino slot club card.
Slot clubs were designed to reward players for their loyalty to that casino. Use of the free slot card—sometimes referred to as a comp card—can result in rewards ranging from free meals, rooms, and shows, to cash rebates. But the card reader is not in any way linked to the random number generator that determines which cards are dealt, so the card will have no effect, either positive or negative, on the game itself.

Myth: The machine deals better cards when you bet the minimum number of coins.
The computer inside the machine doesn't care how much you wager. Regardless of the amount you bet, it will generate a hand at random. Nevertheless, I strongly advise you to always bet the maximum number of coins because if you draw a Royal Flush, you will be paid 800 times your bet *only* if you have bet the maximum. If you wager fewer coins, you will win only 250 times your bet.

Myth: Because the machines are set for a specific payout, it doesn't matter how you play. Regardless of your decision to hold certain cards, the result will be the same, as it's predetermined.
This is the most destructive myth of all. It's true that you can't affect the cards you are dealt, but you *can* affect your final hand by using mathematically proven strategies to choose the cards you will hold. Unlike slots, video poker rewards those who select good games and play those games with skill. Be aware, though, that there are some video poker machines—called video lottery terminals (VLTs)—that choose winning hands ahead of time, making playing strategies useless. You can learn more about VLTs by turning to the inset on page 35.

The programming for the RNG is found on the EPROM (Erasable Programmable Read-Only Memory) computer chip. Contrary to what many people believe, the RNG doesn't actually "shuffle" virtual cards. Instead, it is constantly producing combinations of numbers within a specified range. For instance, in a Jacks or Better game, which uses a fifty-two-card deck, each card has its own number from 1 to 52. (See page 10 for more information on Jacks or Better.) When a triggering event occurs—when coins are inserted, or the *Bet One Credit* or *Bet Max* button is pressed—the microprocessor that controls the machine snatches five random numbers within $\frac{1}{1000}$ of a second. Each of these numbers is then translated into a card image, and the player has her starting hand.

Although all video poker machines deal the first five cards in the way described above, the machines do differ in the way they select replacements for the cards that the player decides to discard. Many video poker machines built before the mid-eighties use a so-called *parallel* method of dealing, in which the machine simultaneously chooses not only the five cards that constitute the hand, but also the five replacement cards for the draw. Each of the five replacement cards is "assigned" to one of the cards in the hand and is lined up behind it—although the alternate card cannot be seen by the player, of course. If and when the player makes the decision to not hold a card, the replacement card is revealed.

When these early video poker machines were introduced, many players objected to parallel dealing because the card they needed to complete a winning hand might be behind a card they held, and therefore unavailable to them. For this reason, between the mid-eighties and the late nineties, casinos began offering video poker machines that used *serial dealing*, so-called because when the machine deals the five-card hand, it also chooses five unseen replacement cards, which are "stacked" sequentially. No matter which card is discarded by the player, the first replacement card in the sequence is revealed; if two cards are discarded, the first two replacements in the sequence are revealed, etc.

Many of the poker machines manufactured after 1996 use a method of dealing replacements different from those discussed above. Called *five and five* dealing, it does not select the replacement cards for the draw when the five-card hand is dealt. Instead, after the deal, the RNG continues to produce number combinations. Only when the player

Video Lottery Terminals

This chapter explains how the random number generator (RNG) deals cards in a way that is just as random as the dealing of cards in a real game. (See page 32 for information on the random number generator.) Once an initial hand is dealt, you can choose to hold some cards, at which point the machine randomly deals replacements for those you did not hold. Clearly, then, the decisions you make when playing a game at these machines *do* affect the final outcome.

Unfortunately, not all video poker machines work this way. Although they look much like regular video poker machines, *video lottery terminals,* or *VLTs,* usually do *not* use a random number generator—although a few of them do. Instead, the majority are programmed to have a predetermined number of winners, much like a paper lottery. Usually, the machine at which you play is not even the one that chooses the winner. Rather, the winner is determined by a central computer that links all the separate VLTs together within either a casino or a jurisdiction.

How will you know if the machine you come across is a VLT, and not a real video poker machine? First, consider if you live in one of the states that allow video lottery terminals. For instance, if you live in a state that does *not* have a lottery, you can feel safe that the casinos have real video poker machines—machines that require skill. Second, keep in mind that most video poker machines in bars, restaurants, trucks stops, and fraternal organizations *are* VLTs. The same is true of the machines in racinos—combination race tracks and casinos. Finally, although it may change, remember that at this point, VLTs are rarely if ever found in commercial (nontribal) casinos. (To learn more about the different types of casinos, turn to Chapter 5.)

As you may have surmised by now, this is a fairly complex issue, and one that is changing all the time. Many states that do not have VLTs are trying to get permission to use them even as I write this book. Moreover, casinos and other establishments with game machines are often unwilling to confirm or deny that their machines are VLTs. Add to this the fact that an establishment may have both VLT and non-VLT machines—neither of which is identified as such—and you can see how hard it is to locate a fair video poker machine in some regions of the country.

To help create some order in this confusion, I have put together Table 2.1, which presents available information on each state, telling you if that state has VLTs and, if so, where they may be located. The table also specifically indicates if certain venues have or may have Class II or Class III video poker machines. Class II video poker machines—which may or may not be called VLTs—do *not* have random number generators, and thus make the use of strategies pointless. Class III video poker game machines may or may not have RNGs, and, like Class II machines, may or may not be called VLTs. The machines in these classes, then, represent a gray area in video poker play, and probably mean that you should look elsewhere—in another type of casino or even another state—for a fair game.

Table 2.1. **Video Lottery Terminals and Class II and III Machines**

State	Does It Have VLTs?	If Yes, Where?
Alabama	Yes.	Tribal casinos have Class II machines.
Alaska	Yes.	Tribal casinos have Class II and Class III machines.
Arizona	No.	
Arkansas	No.	
California	Yes.	Only the Morongo and Pechanga tribal casinos have VLTs.
Colorado	Unknown.	
Connecticut	Yes.	Foxwoods' online "Play Away" game is a VLT. (Foxwoods has regular video poker machines in the actual casino.)
Delaware	Yes.	VLTs are found in racinos.
Florida	Yes.	All tribal video poker games are VLTs.
Georgia	No.	
Hawaii	No.	
Idaho	Unknown.	VLTs might be found in tribal casinos.
Illinois	Unknown.	The state is considering the use of VLTs in racinos.
Indiana	Unknown.	The state is considering the use of VLTs in racinos.
Iowa	Yes.	VLTs are found in racinos and noncasino retailers.*
Kansas	Pending Senate vote.	
Kentucky	Yes.	VLTs are found in noncasino retailers,* although some are illegal and unregulated. The state is considering the use of VLTs in racinos.
Louisiana	Yes.	VLTs are found in racinos and noncasino retailers.*
Maine	Yes.	VLTs are found at Bangor's harness track. Tribes have proposed slots—including video poker—for casinos, but have not yet been approved.
Maryland	Yes.	VLTs are found in the one casino in the state. The state is considering the use of VLTs in racinos.
Massachusetts	Pending final approval.	
Michigan	Yes.	VLTs are found in noncasino retailers,* and might be in tribal casinos as well.

State	Does It Have VLTs?	If Yes, Where?
Minnesota	Unknown.	VLTs might be found in tribal casinos. The state is considering the use of VLTs in bars.
Mississippi	No.	
Missouri	Unknown.	
Montana	Yes.	VLTs are found in noncasino retailers.*
Nebraska	Yes.	Tribal casinos have Class II machines.
Nevada	No.	
New Hampshire	Yes.	VLTs are expected to be installed in dog tracks and racinos.
New Jersey	No.	VLTs have been proposed for the Meadowlands.
New Mexico	Yes.	VLTs are found in racinos, tribal casinos, nonprofit organizations, and noncasino retailers.*
New York	Yes.	VLTs are found in racinos, and have been proposed for the ferry between Rochester and Toronto.
North Carolina	Yes.	VLTs are found in noncasino retailers,* and tribal casinos have Class II machines.
North Dakota	No.	
Ohio	No.	The state is considering the use of VLTs in racinos.
Oklahoma	Yes.	VLTs are found in tribal casinos and racinos.
Oregon	Yes.	VLTs are found in noncasino retailers.*
Pennsylvania	Yes.	VLTs have not yet been installed.
Rhode Island	Yes.	VLTs are found in racinos and Jai Alai Frontons.
South Carolina	Yes.	VLTs are found in noncasino retailers.*
South Dakota	Yes.	VLTs are found in noncasino retailers.*
Tennessee	No.	
Texas	Yes.	Tribal casino has Class II machines, and the state is considering the use of VLTs in racinos.
Utah	No.	
Vermont	No.	

State	Does It Have VLTs?	If Yes, Where?
Virginia	Unknown.	
Washington	Yes.	Although video poker is officially not allowed in the state, VLTs are found in tribal casinos in the form of Class II and Class III machines.
West Virginia	Yes.	VLTs are found in racinos and noncasino retailers.*
Wisconsin	Unknown.	VLTs might be found in tribal casinos.
Wyoming	Unknown.	VLTs might be found in tribal casinos.

* Noncasino retailers include bars, taverns, restaurants, truck stops, and fraternal organizations.

Let's say that you live in a state in which casinos or other businesses are permitted to have video lottery terminals, and you want to know if the specific machine you've found is a regular video poker machine or a VLT. As mentioned earlier, VLTs look like regular video poker machines, so you won't be able to easily use appearance as a guide. However, before you play, you may be able to identify a VLT by checking for certain manufacturing and brand name information on the machine. You will know that a video poker machine is really a VLT if you find the following:

☐ The machine was manufactured by GTECH or Spielo, a subsidiary of GTECH.

☐ The words AURA or Power Station 5 are emblazoned above the display screen, indicating that they're GTECH machines.

☐ The machine was manufactured by Sodak, an IGT subsidiary that makes Class II games.

☐ The machine was manufactured by World Touch Gaming, which makes VLTs for tribal casinos.

Once you actually play a game on a machine, you'll know that it's really a video lottery terminal if one of the following events occurs:

☐ At the end of the game, a genie appears on the display screen and changes the cards.

☐ The machine has a "Match Card" feature that awards bonus credits at the end of the game.

☐ The machine has an "automatic hold" on the buttons that prevents you from selecting the cards that will be held.

☐ The machine deals a final hand without giving you an opportunity to draw new cards.

The bottom line is that because the majority of video lottery terminals do not have random number generators, the "games" they offer are not really games of skill at all, but merely lotteries posing as casino games. No playing strategies presented in this or any other book can work with these machines because the winning "tickets" have been predetermined by a central computer. The best strategy? Once you determine that a machine is a video lottery terminal, keep walking.

decides to hold certain cards does the RNG select replacements for those cards not being held.

Although you are not likely to see any difference between the workings of a video poker machine produced before 1996 and one produced after that year, you might wish to distinguish between the newer and older machines—especially since it's so easy to do so. Very few parallel-dealing machines remain in casinos, but in some casinos, you may find a few that use serial dealing. These older machines are easy to identify because they will accept coins and do *not* have touch screens. As you might expect, the newer machines that use five and five dealing do *not* have coin slots, and *do* have touch screens.

At this point, a few words should be said about the randomness of the random number generator. Many players refuse to believe that the card combinations generated by a video poker machine are random, and point to winning and losing streaks as proof that there is a pattern to the hands. The fact is that outside the field of quantum physics, true randomness is hard to achieve. Nevertheless, the RNG, which uses an algorithm to produce random numbers, results in an amount of predictability so miniscule that it is not discernible. Yes, winning and losing streaks do occur, but the video poker machine is not *programmed* to create these streaks. The streaks simply occur at random, just as streaks occur when you toss a coin and "heads" shows up several times in a row. Therefore, the gambler who has experienced a wave-like roller coaster effect of wins and losses, and believes that he has to ride out the down slope of the wave to follow it back up again, is likely to be disappointed. Betting based on this "wave" idea may appear to work in the short term, but does not work in the long term. The only system that works over time is the use of proven video poker strategies, which you'll find detailed in the next chapter.

Don't let your experience of winning and losing streaks trick you into believing that there is a predictable pattern to the hands produced by the random number generator. Think of a coin toss. Even if you've flipped ten heads in a row, your odds of getting heads on the next toss remain 50/50. The long and short of it is that statistical odds are unchanged by past events, whether those events are coin tosses or video poker hands.

You should now be familiar with the video poker machine, and be able to discriminate a real video poker machine from a video lottery terminal. But if you want to win at video poker, you'll have to know more than the location of the *Hold/Cancel* and *Cash Out* buttons. You'll have to learn how to identify the best games and play them using proven strategies. If you're ready to gain the winning edge in video poker, Chapter 3 will provide you with the information that you seek.

VIDEO POKER STRATEGY

Years ago, I played table games like blackjack, five- and seven-card stud poker, and Texas Hold'em. At the time, these games offered the best chance to win money when they were played correctly. But times have changed, and today it's video poker that offers the best player advantage games available in a casino. Unfortunately, it's also true that there are a lot of bad video poker games out there—games that, in the long run, will give your money to the casino, instead of sending it back home with you. In short, to gain the winning edge in video poker, you have to find the best video poker games and play them correctly. You won't win every time, of course, but if you play smart, you will be ahead in the long run and have fun along the way.

This chapter starts off by explaining some fundamental terms and concepts that will allow you to understand what makes one video poker game better than another. It then guides you through the process of finding the great games described in Chapter 1, and provides you with the strategies needed to play these games successfully.

UNDERSTANDING BASIC PAYOFF-RELATED TERMS AND TOOLS

While someone new to the world of video poker may stroll into a casino, choose the first free video poker machine, and sit down and play the game—whatever that game may be—the knowledgeable player isn't likely to select a machine just because no one else is playing it. Instead, he chooses a machine and a game based on pay tables, expected returns, and other important concepts, all of which relate to the amount of money he can win by playing that game, and the likelihood that a given game will actually yield the winning hand he's looking for. If this sounds a bit complicated, don't worry. The following discussions will build your knowledge of payoff-related terms step by step, until you can confidently walk into any casino and choose the best video poker game that establishment has to offer.

Pay Tables

The *pay table*, which was first discussed in Chapter 1 (see page 9), presents the winning hand combinations for a specific video poker game and lists the payout for each combination. Specifically, the table shows how many *coins* are returned for each winning hand based on the number of coins bet. In this book, I have included pay tables for all the games I recommend, and for convenience, have stated the game's expected return below each table title. You will learn about the expected return later in the chapter, on page 48. For the time being, just remember that this piece of information is *not* included in casino pay tables.

Table 3.1. **Pay Table for 9/6 Jacks or Better**
Expected Return: 99.54%

Winning Hand	I coin	2 coins	3 coins	4 coins	5 coins
Royal Flush	250	500	750	1000	4000
Straight Flush	50	100	150	200	250
Four of a Kind	25	50	75	100	125
Full House	9	18	27	36	45
Flush	6	12	18	24	30
Straight	4	8	12	16	20
Three of a Kind	3	6	9	12	15
Two Pair	2	4	6	8	10
Jacks or Better	1	2	3	4	5

To better understand the significance of the pay table, look at Table 3.1, which presents the pay table for 9/6 Jacks or Better, one of the eight games recommended in Chapter 1. While for the most part, Table 3.1 is self-explanatory, a few features should be pointed out. First note that if you bet 1 coin and have a winning hand of Jacks or Better—in other words, a pair of Jacks, Queens, Kings, or Aces—1 coin is returned to you. In other words, even though Jacks or Better is a winning hand, you only break even, winning what is called *even money*. However, as you move up the hierarchy of hands, the return improves for each 1-coin bet. If you draw Two Pair and bet 1 coin, for instance, you get a 2-coin return. If you draw Three of a Kind and bet 1 coin, you get a 3-coin return, and so on.

Now let's go back to the Two Pair hand and see what happens as you increase the *size* of your bet. As already stated, if you bet 1 coin, you get a 2-coin return for this hand. For a 2-coin bet, you receive 4 coins (2 x 2 = 4); for a 3-coin bet, 6 coins (3 x 2 = 6), and so on. This basic pattern is used to calculate returns for almost every winning combination. You get a certain number of coins—a specific return—for a 1-coin bet, and for each wager, that return is multiplied by the number of coins bet to determine the payout. But when you draw the highest winning hand, the Royal Flush, something interesting occurs. That hand returns 250 coins for each 1-coin bet *until you make a 5-coin bet*. For that wager, instead of receiving the expected 1,250 coins (5 x 250 = 1,250), you receive 800 coins for every coin bet, for a total of 4,000 coins. If this is confusing to you, Table 3.2—which shows the returns for the Royal Flush for various bets—should help.

The pay table, which is found on every video poker machine, shows how many coins are returned for each winning hand based on the number of coins bet. Reading these tables is a must, as they will enable you to identify those games with the best payoffs.

Table 3.2. Coin Returns for Royal Flush Combination in 9/6 Jacks or Better

Number of Coins Bet	Number of Coins Returned for Each Coin Bet	Total Coins Returned
1	250	250
2	250	500
3	250	750
4	250	1,000
5	800	4,000

What can you learn from this? When playing video poker, to gain the winning edge, you should always play the maximum number of coins—usually, 5 coins. If you don't, in most cases you will not get the best payback for a Royal Flush. Moreover, unless you wager maximum coins, you will not be eligible for a progressive jackpot. (To learn about the progressive jackpot, see page 63.) If betting maximum coins is beyond your means for a particular game, I advise you to go down a denomination, playing a nickel game instead of a quarter game, for instance. In most cases, you will lose your advantage by playing less than max coins.

On the following pages, you'll find pay tables for the seven other video poker games recommended in Chapter 1. If you find yourself confused by some of the payoffs—by the unusually high payoff for certain odd combinations in Double Double Bonus Poker, for instance—you may want to turn back to Chapter 1, which provides a brief description of each game, as well as insights into any unusual payoffs. Chapter 1 also explains concepts such as the Wild Royal Flush and discusses several other winning hands that can puzzle a newcomer to the world of video poker.

The pay table is not always displayed on a video poker machine when you first walk up to it. To learn how to gain access to pay tables on different types of machines, see page 26 of Chapter 2.

If you skipped over Chapter 2, which explains the physical setup of the video poker machine, you also may want to flip back to that chapter to learn how you can gain access to the pay table. In brief, on older single-game machines, the pay table is sometimes displayed on the manufacturer's glass—the piece of glass on which the name of the game is also emblazoned. On newer single-game machines, you'll see the pay table on the display screen when you first walk up to the machine. On a multi-game or multi-hand machine, you must first make a selection from a menu of different games and, in some cases, a menu of denominations. At that point, the pay table for the chosen game is displayed on the machine.

Never forget that if you want the winning edge in video poker, it is crucial to match up the pay table found on the video poker machine with the table for the exact game you want. Not every game of Deuces Wild gives you the generous payoffs shown in Table 3.6, nor does every game of Double Double Bonus Poker provide the excellent returns listed in Table 3.4. A smart use of pay tables will guide you to *full-pay games*—video poker games that will give you the best possible return on your bet.

Table 3.3. **Pay Table for 8/5 Bonus Poker**
Expected Return: 99.17%

Winning Hand	I coin	2 coins	3 coins	4 coins	5 coins
Royal Flush	250	500	750	1000	4000
Straight Flush	50	100	150	200	250
Four Aces	80	160	240	320	400
Four Twos, Threes, or Fours	40	80	120	160	200
Four Fives to Kings	25	50	75	100	125
Full House	8	16	24	32	40
Flush	5	10	15	20	25
Straight	4	8	12	16	20
Three of a Kind	3	6	9	12	15
Two Pair	2	4	6	8	10
Jacks or Better	1	2	3	4	5

Table 3.4. **Pay Table for 9/6 Double Double Bonus Poker**
Expected Return: 98.98%

Winning Hand	I coin	2 coins	3 coins	4 coins	5 coins
Royal Flush	250	500	750	1000	4000
Straight Flush	50	100	150	200	250
Four Aces with a Two, Three, or Four	400	800	1200	1600	2000
Four Twos, Threes, or Fours, with an Ace, Two, Three, or Four	160	320	480	640	800
Four Aces	160	320	480	640	800
Four Twos, Threes, or Fours	80	160	240	320	400
Four Fives to Kings	50	100	150	200	250
Full House	9	18	27	36	45
Flush	6	12	18	24	30
Straight	4	8	12	16	20
Three of a Kind	3	6	9	12	15
Two Pair	1	2	3	4	5
Jacks or Better	1	2	3	4	5

Table 3.5.   **Pay Table for 9/6 Bonus Poker Deluxe**
Expected Return: 99.64%

Winning Hand	1 coin	2 coins	3 coins	4 coins	5 coins
Royal Flush	250	500	750	1000	4000
Straight Flush	50	100	150	200	250
Four of a Kind	80	160	240	320	400
Full House	9	18	27	36	45
Flush	6	12	18	24	30
Straight	4	8	12	16	20
Three of a Kind	3	6	9	12	15
Two Pair	1	2	3	4	5
Jacks or Better	1	2	3	4	5

Table 3.6.   **Pay Table for Full-Pay Deuces Wild**
Expected Return: 100.76%

Winning Hand	1 coin	2 coins	3 coins	4 coins	5 coins
Royal Flush	250	500	750	1000	4000
Four Deuces	200	400	600	800	1000
Wild Royal Flush	25	50	75	100	125
Five of a Kind	15	30	45	60	75
Straight Flush	9	18	27	36	45
Four of a Kind	5	10	15	20	25
Full House	3	6	9	12	15
Flush	2	4	6	8	10
Straight	2	4	6	8	10
Three of a Kind	1	2	3	4	5

Table 3.7.   **Pay Table for Not-So-Ugly Deuces Wild**
Expected Return: 99.73%

Winning Hand	1 coin	2 coins	3 coins	4 coins	5 coins
Royal Flush	250	500	750	1000	4000
Four Deuces	200	400	600	800	1000
Wild Royal Flush	25	50	75	100	125
Five of a Kind	16	32	48	64	80

Straight Flush	10	20	30	40	50
Four of a Kind	4	8	12	16	20
Full House	4	8	12	16	20
Flush	3	6	9	12	15
Straight	2	4	6	8	10
Three of a Kind	1	2	3	4	5

Table 3.8. **Pay Table for 10/7 Double Bonus Poker**
Expected Return: 100.17%

Winning Hand	1 coin	2 coins	3 coins	4 coins	5 coins
Royal Flush	250	500	750	1000	4000
Straight Flush	50	100	150	200	250
Four Aces	160	320	480	640	800
Four Twos, Threes, or Fours	80	160	240	320	400
Four Fives to Kings	50	100	150	200	250
Full House	10	20	30	40	50
Flush	7	14	21	28	35
Straight	5	10	15	20	25
Three of a Kind	3	6	9	12	15
Two Pair	1	2	3	4	5
Jacks or Better	1	2	3	4	5

Table 3.9. **Pay Table for Full-Pay Pick'Em Poker**
Expected Return: 99.95%

Winning Hand	1 coin	2 coins	3 coins	4 coins	5 coins
Royal Flush	1000	2000	3000	4000	6000
Straight Flush	200	400	600	800	1199
Four of a Kind	100	200	300	400	600
Full House	18	36	54	72	90
Flush	15	30	45	60	75
Straight	11	22	33	44	55
Three of a Kind	5	10	15	20	25
Two Pair	3	6	9	12	15
Nines or Better	2	4	6	8	10

Pay Charts

Now that you understand how to locate and read the pay table for each video poker game, you've taken an important step towards gaining the winning edge in video poker. After all, one of the most important strategies is choosing the best video poker game available. But unfortunately, it's not practical to carry around a stack of pay tables. That's why I devised the *pay chart,* which is an abbreviated version of a pay table that includes an additional piece of information called the expected return. Through use of the pay chart—which is only two lines long, allowing a number of charts to fit on a single card or sheet of paper—you can determine whether a given video poker game is a player advantage game or a casino advantage game. But before we discuss the setup of a pay chart, you have to understand what an expected return is.

The Expected Return

The expected return, or ER, applies only to games played on machines with random number generators (RNGs). It cannot be applied to games played on a video lottery terminal (VLT), as these machines do not have random number generators. (See page 32 for information about the random number generator, and page 35 for a discussion of the video lottery machine.)

The expected return, or ER, is the theoretical return you can expect from a game if you play it correctly for the long run—in other words, for many hands. The more hands played over time, the closer the actual results will conform to the statistical expectation. Most experts agree that *millions* of hands make up a reasonable approximation of "the long run."

Expressed as a percentage, the ER is determined by comparing the number of coins bet to the number of coins won for each winning hand in that game. This means that if the odds of receiving a specific winning combination were identical to the payout for the combination throughout the game, the ER would be 100%. For example, if the odds of a hand occurring are one out of four and the game pays you four times the bet for the hand, the ER is 100%. Be aware that because the expected return—also called the *payback percentage*—is based on the pay table, any changes whatsoever in the pay table will change the ER for that game.

The calculations needed to determine the ER are very complex, and require the use of a video poker software training program. (You'll learn about these on page 82.) Fortunately, you will not have to compute the ER for the video poker games in this book, since I have calculated them for you and included them in the pay tables presented on pages 42 and 45 to 47, and the pay charts shown on pages 54 to 56. However, it is important to understand how to use the ER to determine the amount of money you will theoretically have after playing a particular game for a specific amount of time. Here's how to calculate your return in terms of dollars:

1. Convert the ER for that game from a percentage to a decimal. Do this by moving the decimal point two places to the left and dropping the percent sign.

2. Multiply the resulting decimal by the total amount of your wager.

To see how this two-step process works, let's assume that you want to predict the theoretical results of wagering a total of $250 on Full-Pay Deuces Wild, which has an ER of 100.76%. (See the pay table on page 46.) To determine your theoretical return in dollars:

1. Convert 100.76% to a decimal by moving the decimal point two places to the left and dropping the percent sign. The result is 1.0076.

2. Multiply 1.0076 by your total wager, which is $250. The result is $251.90.

What does this mean? It means that if you play Full-Pay Deuces Wild with perfect or nearly perfect strategies for a long enough period of time, you can expect to win $1.90 for every $250 you bet. ($251.90 − $250.00 = $1.90)

Now, let's take the same wager but this time play 9/6 Double Double Bonus Poker, which has an expected return of 98.98%. What would your theoretical return be in cash?

1. Convert 98.98% to a decimal by moving the decimal point two places to the left and dropping the percent sign. The result is .9898.

2. Multiply .9898 by your total wager, which is $250. The result is $247.45. In other words, you can expect to lose $2.55 for every $250 you wager. ($250 − $247.45 = $2.55)

Be aware that your total wager—called *coin-in*—is found by adding all of the amounts you bet together. If you were to play just 600 hands per hour on a quarter machine—which would mean you were playing at a relatively slow pace—you would have a total coin-in of $250 after just twenty minutes of play.

As you can see, you can expect to lose money when the ER is less than 100%, and you can expect to win money when the ER is greater than 100%. Games that return less than 100% are therefore called *casino advantage games* because the games favor the casino. Games that return more than 100% are called *player advantage games* because the games favor the player. They are also referred to as *positive games.*

As I've already mentioned, the actual return is more likely to resemble the ER as the number of hands is increased—and then, only with nearly perfect play. Anything is possible in the short term. With short play, you can lose money at a player advantage game or win money at a casino advantage game. But over the long term, assuming accurate play, the best game is the one with the highest ER.

Should you ever play a casino advantage game? Sometimes a game with an ER of less than 100% becomes a player advantage game due to progressive jackpots, which are discussed later in the chapter (see page 63). Cash back offers and other casino promotions, which will be discussed in Chapter 5, can also turn a negative game into a positive one. But if a game has a very low ER, even cash back offers and progressives will not compensate, and you will lose money.

Finally, it's worth pointing out that the earlier scenarios, which involved a total coin-in of only $250, were not realistic. Even if you play only a relatively low denomination like quarters, and even if you play for only an hour, your total coin-in will be considerably higher than $250. It's important to understand that video poker is a fast-paced game that involves making a large number of wagers in a short amount of time. That's one of the many reasons it's important to choose a machine with the highest ER available.

The Expected Value

You now should understand why it's so important to examine pay tables and use the expected return—a percentage based on pay tables—to wisely select a video poker game. But as you learned in earlier chapters, any one game may be offered in several denominations, ranging from pennies to $500. Although the denominations available on a given machine tend to be limited, if you look at different machines, you will see $.01, $.05, $.10, $.25, $.50, $1, $2, $5, $10, $25, $100, and $500 video poker choices. Most casinos place the higher denomination machines—$5 and up—in a special "high roller" room. Keep in mind that when selecting the machine you want to play, you must multiply the denomination by 5—the maximum coin bet for most games—to compute actual bets. In other words, if you are playing a single-hand $5 machine, each bet should be $25—not $5. Also, many machines are multi-hand, meaning you will play up to a hundred hands at the same time. (See the inset on multi-hand video poker machines on page 30.) How should you choose the best denomination to play? That's what the expected value is all about.

The *expected value,* or *EV,* is the amount of money you should be ahead after playing a positive game for a specific amount of time. It is based on the expected return and the amount you are wagering. Although you will most likely play for more than an hour, it's helpful to compute the EV for a one-hour interval—especially when using it to compare different games or the same game played for different wagers. Here's how to compute the expected value:

1. Multiply the cost of each hand by the total number of hands you intend to play during an hour. You now have the total coin-in—your total wager—for a one-hour session.

2. Convert the ER for that game from a percentage to a decimal by moving the decimal point two places to the left and dropping the percent sign.

3. Multiply the resulting decimal by the total coin-in to determine your return in terms of cash.

4. Subtract the total amount of your wager determined in Step 1 from your total return determined in Step 3 to calculate your theoretical win—your expected value.

Let's see how these calculations can help you determine your theoretical win for two games that have different ERs and are played on machines of different denominations. We will then compare the two EVs to see which game has the highest theoretical return.

Let's first consider the EV for Full-Pay Deuces Wild, which has an ER of 100.76%. Let's assume that you are playing quarters, and are bet-

When searching for a low-denomination video poker machine, take a good look at any "penny" machine before you decide to play it. You'll find that most of them are multi-hand machines, which means that your wager, although small, will be multiplied by the number of hands you play for each game.

ting maximum coins for a total wager per hand of $1.25. Let's further assume you have determined that you play 700 hands in an hour.

1. Multiply $1.25, the cost of each hand, by 700, the total number of hands. The result is $875.

2. Convert the game's ER, 100.76%, to a decimal by moving the decimal point two places to the left and dropping the percent sign. The result is 1.0076.

3. Multiply 1.0076 by $875. The result is $881.65. This is your return.

4. Subtract $875 (your wager) from $881.65 (your return). The result, $6.65, is your EV—your theoretical win for an hour of play.

Now let's say that you're considering playing a different game—10/7 Double Bonus Poker—but at a $5 machine. Since you are again betting maximum coins, each hand costs $25. The ER is 100.17% and you are playing 700 hands an hour.

1. Multiply $25, the cost of each hand, by 700, the total number of hands. The result is $17,500.

2. Convert the game's ER, 100.17%, to a decimal by moving the decimal point two places to the left and dropping the percent sign. The result is 1.0017.

3. Multiply 1.0017 by $17,500. The result is $17,529.75. This is your return.

4. Subtract $17,500 (your wager) from $17,529.75 (your return). The result, $29.75, is your EV—your theoretical win for an hour of play.

If you find yourself confusing the term ER with the term EV, remember that the ER (expected return) is a percentage, and the EV (expected value) is an amount of money.

As you can see, even though Full-Pay Deuces Wild has a higher ER (100.76%) than 10/7 Double Bonus (100.17%), the EV for 10/7 Double Bonus is higher. In fact, for each hour of play, you can expect to win $23.10 more playing Double Bonus Poker than you would playing Full-Pay Deuces wild in the denominations specified. ($29.75 – $6.65 = $23.10.) In this case, the higher denomination—five dollars versus a quarter—makes the difference. But sometimes a lower-denomination machine has the best ER. Is there, then, no rule of thumb when choosing denominations? In general, when playing a casino advantage game, which has an ER below 100 percent, you'll want to choose the lowest denomination possible, as this will reduce your losses. What if casino promotions turn a casino advantage game into a player advantage game? In that case, by all means go for the higher denomination machine.

One final point should be made about using expected value to select a game. Unless you are a professional video poker player, when choosing a game, you have to consider not just the math, but also your gambling budget. Chapter 4 will fill you in on some sound money management techniques that will help you both establish and stick to a budget.

Understanding Pay Charts

Now that you've learned some basic terms as well as a number of useful calculations, it's time to return to the subject first introduced on page 48—the pay chart. As explained earlier, the pay chart combines an abbreviated form of a game's pay table with its expected return, giving you the information you need to make a smart choice of video poker games. Specifically, the pay chart gives you the per-coin return both for 1 coin and 5 coins. Why? As you learned earlier in the chapter, to get the best payback for a Royal Flush, you must play the maximum number of coins—usually, 5 coins. Moreover, the expected return given for each game is correct only if you play the maximum number of coins. I included the 1-coin return as well to make the match easier when you are in the casino, particularly if you come across a 10-coin maximum game. In that case, the 1-coin amounts will be the same, but you'll have to play 10 coins if you want to receive the expected return indicated on the pay chart.

If you find the idea of the pay chart confusing, look at Table 3.10, which reprints the pay table for the full-pay version of Jacks or Better shown earlier in the chapter, but shades all of the information that will appear on the pay chart for this game. Once you've examined the pay table, look at the two-line pay chart below. Note that while the pay table starts with the highest winning hand, the pay chart starts with the lowest winning hand.

Jacks or Better: 1 coin: 1-2-3-4-6-9-25-50-25-50-250

5-coins: 5-10-15-20-30-45-125-250-4000. . . 99.54%, Full-Pay

Table 3.10.   **Pay Table for 9/6 Jacks or Better**
              Expected Return: 99.54%

Winning Hand	1 coin	2 coins	3 coins	4 coins	5 coins
Royal Flush	250	500	750	1000	4000
Straight Flush	50	100	150	200	250
Four of a Kind	25	50	75	100	125
Full House	9	18	27	36	45
Flush	6	12	18	24	30
Straight	4	8	12	16	20
Three of a Kind	3	6	9	12	15
Two Pair	2	4	6	8	10
Jacks or Better	1	2	3	4	5

Table 3.11 provides the pay charts for different versions of the games explained in Chapter 1. Note that I don't recommend all of these versions; I strongly advise you to stick to the full-pay form of each game, which you'll be able to identify in the following table by looking for the word "Yes" in the right-hand column "Best Game?" But these charts can help you evaluate games that you're likely to find at casinos and quickly home in on the best ones available. (Note that pay charts for common games *not* described in Chapter 1 can be found on page 136.)

Table 3.11.   **Pay Charts for Common Video Poker Games**

Jacks or Better		
Coin Payoffs	**Expected Return***	**Best Game? (Full Pay)**
1 coin: 1-2-3-4-5-6-25-50-250 5 coins: 5-10-15-20-25-30-125-250-4000	95.00%	No
1 coin: 1-2-3-4-5-7-25-50-250 5 coins: 5-10-15-20-25-35-125-250-4000	96.15%	No
1 coin: 1-2-3-4-5-8-25-50-250 5 coins: 5-10-15-20-25-40-125-250-4000	97.30%	No
1 coin: 1-2-3-4-6-8-25-50-250 5 coins: 5-10-15-20-30-40-125-250-4000	98.39%	No

Coin Payoffs	Expected Return*	Best Game? (Full Pay)
I coin: 1-2-3-4-5-9-25-50-250 5 coins: 5-10-15-20-25-45-125-250-4000	98.45%	No
I coin: 1-2-3-4-5-8-30-50-250 5 coins: 5-10-15-20-25-40-150-250-4000	98.48%	No
I coin: 1-2-3-4-6-9-25-50-250 5 coins: 5-10-15-20-30-45-125-250-4000	99.54%	Yes

Bonus Poker Deluxe		
Coin Payoffs	**Expected Return***	**Best Game? (Full Pay)**
I coin: 1-1-3-4-5-7-80-50-250 5 coins: 5-5-15-20-25-35-400-250-4000	96.25%	No
I coin: 1-1-3-4-5-8-80-50-250 5 coins: 5-5-15-20-25-40-400-250-4000	97.40%	No
I coin: 1-1-3-4-6-8-80-50-250/4,000 5 coins: 5-5-15-20-30-40-400-250-4000	98.49%	No
I coin: 1-1-3-4-6-9-80-50-250 5 coins: 5-5-15-20-30-45-400-250-4000	99.64%	Yes

Deuces Wild[†]		
Coin Payoffs	**Expected Return***	**Best Game? (Full Pay)**
I coin: 1-2-2-3-5-9-15-25-200-250 5 coins: 5-10-10-15-25-45-75-125-1000-4000	100.76%	Yes
I coin: 1-2-3-4-4-10-16-25-200-250 5 coins: 5-10-15-20-20-50-80-125-1000-4000	99.73%	Yes

Bonus Poker		
Coin Payoffs	**Expected Return***	**Best Game? (Full Pay)**
I coin: 1-1-3-5-8-10-25-40-80-50-250 5 coins: 5-5-15-25-40-50-125-200-400-250-4000	94.18%	No
I coin: 1-2-3-4-5-6-25-40-80-50-250 5 coins: 5-10-15-20-25-30-125-200-400-250-4000	96.87%	No
I coin: 1-2-3-4-5-7-25-40-80-50-250 5 coins: 5-10-15-20-25-35-125-200-400-250-4000	98.01%	No

* For each game, the expected return (ER) has been rounded to the nearest hundredth. To get that ER, you must play the 5-coin maximum.

† Both games of Deuces Wild are marked "Full Pay" because they are actually two different games, both of which pay well. The first (uppermost) game listed is Full-Pay Deuces Wild; the second (lower) game listed is Not-So-Ugly Deuces Wild.

Coin Payoffs	Expected Return*	Best Game? (Full Pay)
1 coin: 1-2-3-4-5-8-30-30-30-50-250 5 coins: 5-10-15-20-25-40-150-150-150-250-4000	98.48%	No
1 coin: 1-2-3-4-5-8-25-40-80-50-250 5 coins: 5-10-15-20-25-40-125-200-400-250-4000	99.17%	Yes

Double Bonus Poker		
Coin Payoffs	Expected Return*	Best Game? (Full Pay)
1 coin: 1-1-3-4-5-8-50-80-160-50-250 5 coins: 5-5-15-20-25-40-250-400-800-250-4000	94.19%	No
1 coin: 1-1-3-5-6-10-50-80-160-50-250 5 coins: 5-5-15-25-30-50-250-400-800-250-4000	98.88%	No
1 coin: 1-1-3-5-7-10-50-80-160-50-250 5 coins: 5-5-15-25-35-50-250-400-800-250-4000	100.17%	Yes

Double Double Bonus Poker		
Coin Payoffs	Expected Return*	Best Game? (Full Pay)
1 coin: 1-1-3-4-5-6-50-80-160-160-400-50-250 5 coins: 5-5-15-20-25-30-250-400-800-800-2000-250-4000	94.66%	No
1 coin: 1-1-3-4-5-8-50-80-160-160-400-50-250 5 coins: 5-5-15-20-25-40-250-400-800-800-2000-250-4000	96.79%	No
1 coin: 1-1-3-4-6-9-50-80-160-160-320-50-250 5 coins: 5-5-15-20-30-45-250-400-800-800-1600-250-4000	98.49%	No
1 coin: 1-1-3-4-6-9-50-80-160-160-400-50-250 5 coins: 5-5-15-20-30-45-250-400-800-800-2000-250-4000	98.98%	Yes

Pick'Em Poker[‡]		
Coin Payoffs	Expected Return*	Best Game? (Full Pay)
1 coin: 2-3-4-10-15-18-100-200-1000 5 coins: 10-15-20-50-75-90-600-1199-6000	96.45%	No
1 coin: 2-3-4-11-15-18-100-200-1000 5 coins: 10-15-20-55-75-90-600-1199-6000	96.95%	No
1 coin: 2-3-5-11-15-18-100-200-1000 5 coins: 10-15-25-55-75-90-600-1199-6000	99.95%	Yes

* For each game, the expected return (ER) has been rounded to the nearest hundredth. To get that ER, you must play the 5-coin maximum.

‡ In Pick'Em Poker, three hands—Four of a Kind, Straight Flush, and Royal Flush—are shorted if you fail to play maximum coins.

What If the Game's Pay Table Doesn't Match Your Pay Chart?

Although throughout this book, I urge you to play the best-paying versions of a few select video poker games, you will sometimes be unable to find your game of choice, and instead will be faced with a different version of the game you want— a lower-paying version of Jacks or Better, for instance. Fortunately, with the use of the pay charts just presented, it is easy to approximate the expected return of the version you have located.

Usually, when comparing a pay chart to a pay table with slightly different payouts, most of the differences are found in the Full House and Flush payouts. These changes can have a major impact on the ER. To compensate, when dealing with non-wild card games, simply add 1.1 percent to the ER for every extra coin payout for either hand, and subtract 1.1 percent from the ER for every coin shortage for either hand.

For example, let's say you're looking for a machine that has 9/6 Jacks or Better. The pay chart for that game is as follows:

1 coin: 1-2-3-4-**6-9**-25-50-250

5-coins: 5-10-15-20-30-45-125-250-4000 . . . 99.54%

While you can't find a game that matches the above pay chart, you find another version of Jacks or Better with the following payoffs:

1 coin: 1-2-3-4-**5-8**-25-50-250

5-coins: 5-10-15-20-25-40-125-250-4000 . . . ?

Your job is to find the expected return for the new game. As you can see by comparing the payoffs, both the Full House and the Flush are one coin shorter in the new game. (See the boldface numerals above.) The Full House is 8 instead of 9, and the Flush is 5 instead of 6. Together, then, the new game is 2 coins short. Using your formula, you subtract 2.2 from the original game's ER—1.1 for each coin shortage—and find that the new game has an ER of approximately 97.32 percent. (99.54% – 2.2% = 97.34%)

While this is just an approximation, you'll find that it is very close to the true ER—which in this case is 97.30 percent—and can help you

The Name of the Game

Coyote Ugly Deuces. Not-So-Ugly Deuces Wild. Full-Pay Pick'Em Poker. 9/6 Jacks or Better. If you talk to experienced video poker players, these are just some of the games they're likely to mention. But you won't find any of these names printed on video poker machines. Why? Because they weren't given to the various games by the manufacturers or the casinos, but by the players themselves.

While this may seem confusing, you can learn a lot about a game from the descriptive name bestowed on it by fellow players. What, for instance, do you think players are saying when they choose a name like Coyote Ugly? If you guessed that this isn't a player advantage game, you're right. As you learned in Chapter 1, the term "Full-Pay" indicates that this version of the game gives you the best possible return on your bets. Chapter 1 also explained that names which include 9/6, 8/5, etc. are telling you something about the game's payoff for certain winning hands. Jacks or Better 9/6, for instance, returns 9 coins on each 1-coin bet if you have a Full House, and 6 coins on each 1-coin bet if you have a Flush.

How can you find a game like Not-So-Ugly Deuces Wild if the name doesn't appear on the video poker machine? By now, you should know the answer: Simply compare the pay table or pay chart for the desired game with the pay tables on the Deuces Wild machines you find in the casino. When you can make a perfect match, you'll know you've found your game.

Why learn which games have high volatility? Games that are highly volatile require a larger bankroll, and should generally be avoided by players with small budgets.

decide if it would be worthwhile to play the game you've found, or if you should keep looking until you locate a better-paying game.

Game Volatility

Before we leave the subject of payoff-related terms, there's another term with which you should be familiar: Volatility. *Volatility* is the likelihood that any individual result will vary greatly from the expected result, or average—the expected return. In other words, it shows how likely you are to achieve the expected return (ER) each time you play a hand. A video poker game whose expected return relies on a few big wins from rare hands is said to have high volatility because during actual play, most hands will fall short of the expected return. A game whose expected return relies on smaller wins from more common hands is said to have low volatility because during play, many more hands will approach the expected return. Figures 3.1 and 3.2 clarify this concept. As you can see, a high-volatility game—shown in Figure 3.1—provides few hands that allow you to break even or win, but occasionally provides a big pot. A low-volatility game—shown in Figure 3.2—gives you more frequent opportunities to win small pots, enabling you to stay in the game longer.

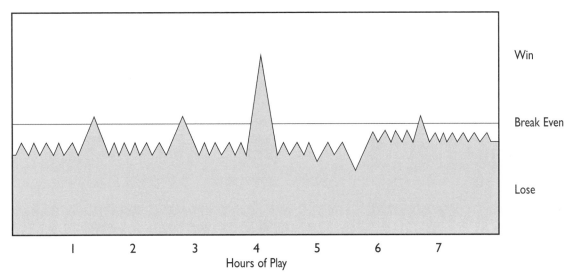

Figure 3.1. **High-Volatility Game**

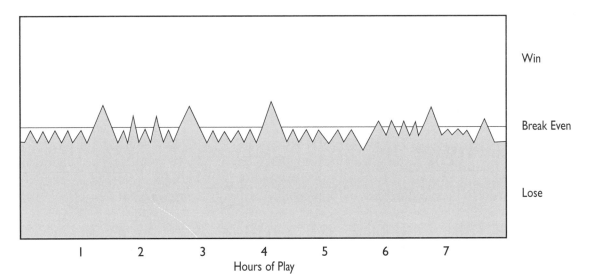

Figure 3.2. **Low-Volatility Game**

It's fairly easy to judge the volatility of a game by looking at its pay table. If you notice high payouts for hands at the top of the pay table as well as short payouts for hands at the bottom of the table, you will know the game is volatile. In non-deuces-wild games, pay particular attention to Two Pair. If you get just even money for that hand, instead of double your money, the game is volatile. In deuces-wild games, if there is a high payout for both the Royal Flush (4,000 coins or more) and Four Deuces (2000 coins or more), the game is volatile.

If you want a more precise measure of a game's volatility, you can determine its variance. *Variance* is the average of the square of the deviation from the mean—in this case, the expected return—and so gives a number to the concept of volatility. The higher the variance, the higher the volatility. Video poker training software, discussed later in the chapter, can compute the variance for any game. Table 3.12, however, presents the variance of every game I recommend in this book.

Table 3.12. The Variance of Recommended Video Poker Games

Game	Variance
9/6 Jacks or Better	19.51
9/6 Bonus Poker Deluxe	32.13
Full-Pay Deuces Wild	25.83
Not-So-Ugly Deuces Wild	25.78
8/5 Bonus Poker	20.90
10/7 Double Bonus Poker	28.26
9/6 Double Double Bonus Poker	41.98
Full-Pay Pick 'Em Poker	15.01

Why would you want a measure of a video poker game's volatility? The fact is that sometimes you should consider more than just the ER to select the best game. A game may have a high ER, but if it also has high volatility, you may lose your bankroll before you hit one of the rare hands that actually pays well.

Table 3.13 contrasts two games—Loose Deuces Wild and Not-So-Ugly Deuces Wild—with respect to volatility. Although Loose Deuces has a higher ER (100.15%) than Not-So-Ugly Deuces (99.73%), as you can see, Loose Deuces Wild is a highly volatile game with a variance of

Table 3.13. **Comparing the Volatility of Loose Deuces Wild and Not-So-Ugly Deuces Wild**

Hand	Loose Deuces Wild Variance: 70.70 Expected Return: 100.15%	Not-So-Ugly Deuces Wild Variance: 25.78 Expected Return: 99.73%	Game Comparison
Royal Flush	4,000 (5-coin payout) 1.78% ER	4,000 (5-coin payout) 1.84% ER	Rare hand. Games have similar ER reliance.
Four Deuces	2,500 (5-coin payout) 10.72% ER	1,000 (5-coin payout) 3.73% ER	Rare hand. Loose Deuces has greater ER reliance.
Royal Flush With Deuces	125 (5-coin payout) 4.27% ER	125 (5-coin payout) 4.77% ER	Less rare hand. Games have similar ER reliance.
Five of a Kind	75 (5-coin payout) 4.78% ER	80 (5-coin payout) 4.97% ER	Less rare hand. Games have similar ER reliance.
Straight Flush	40 (5-coin payout) 3.10% ER	50 (5-coin payout) 5.14% ER	Less Rare Not-So-Ugly Deuces has greater ER reliance.
Four of a Kind	20 (5-coin payout) 26.17% ER	20 (5-coin payout) 24.42% ER	Frequent hand Games have similar ER reliance.
Full House	15 (5-coin payout) 6.36% ER	20 (5-coin payout) 10.45% ER	Frequent hand. Not-So-Ugly Deuces has greater ER reliance.
Flush	10 (5-coin payout) 3.25% ER	15 (5-coin payout) 6.23% ER	Frequent hand. Not-So-Ugly Deuces has greater ER reliance.
Straight	10 (5-coin payout) 11.20% ER	10 (5-coin payout) 11.47% ER	Frequent hand. Games have similar ER reliance.
Three of a Kind	5 (5-coin payout) 28.51% ER	5 (5-coin payout) 26.72% ER	Frequent hand. Games have similar ER reliance.

70.70, while Not-So-Ugly has a variance of only 25.78. The table shows why. The second and third columns each provide the variance and ER for one of the two games, along with the payout for a 5-coin-wager on each winning hand, and—most important—the percentage of the ER that comes from that hand. You can see that Loose Deuces Wild gets 1.78% of its expected return from the Royal Flush, and 10.72% of its return from Four Deuces. It therefore gets 12.5% of its return from the two rarest hands. (1.78 + 10.72 = 12.5) Failure to draw one of these rare hands would result in an expected return of only 87.65%. (100.15 – 12.5 = 87.65) That's why Loose Deuces Wild is considered a volatile, high-risk game. Not-So-Ugly Deuces Wild gets 1.84% of its expected return from the Royal Flush and 3.73% of its return from Four Deuces. It therefore gets 5.57% of its return from the two rarest hands. (1.84 + 3.73 = 5.57) Failure to draw one of these rare hands would result in an expected return of 94.16%. (99.73 – 5.57 = 94.16)

Should you avoid high-volatility games like Loose Deuces Wild? Not necessarily. If the game has a good expected return, you know how to play it, and you have a sizeable bankroll, it might be a good choice for you. Just be aware that you will probably have a bumpy ride on the road to the big payout.

CHOOSING THE GAME

If you read Chapter 1, you know that I recommend eight video poker games. These games include:

❏ 9/6 Jacks or Better

❏ 9/6 Bonus Poker Deluxe

❏ Full-Pay Deuces Wild

❏ Not-So-Ugly Deuces Wild

❏ 8/5 Bonus Poker

❏ 10/7 Double Bonus Poker

❏ 9/6 Double Double Bonus Poker

❏ Full-Pay Pick 'Em Poker

I chose these particular games because they are available in many casinos, they offer excellent expected returns, and they are easy to play with the strategy cards included in this book. But I know that every player has his own goals when choosing a game. So you'll want to consider your reason for playing before selecting your game.

Many players understandably want the best-paying game available. If you share that goal, you'll want to pick games with great paybacks, such as 10/7 Double Bonus Poker. Another money-smart alternative is to choose a game whose value has been increased by casino promotions. Games like Pick'Em Poker and Not-So-Ugly Deuces Wild have ERs close to but slightly under 100%, with Pick 'Em having an ER of 99.95% and Not-So-Ugly having an ER of 99.73%. But as you'll learn in Chapter 5, casino perks can make a significant difference, giving the player the advantage.

Some players are less concerned with payback than they are with having a great time. They love the adrenaline rush experienced when playing a game with dramatic ups and downs. In other words, they want a game with high volatility. (See the discussion of volatility on page 58.) If you count yourself among those who play primarily for fun and excitement, look for a game like Bonus Poker Deluxe or Double Double Bonus Poker, both of which are relatively high-risk games with big payoffs for rare hands. Just don't be so blinded by the promise of fun that you choose a game that has bad returns, or one that you don't know how to play. Winning is always more fun than losing.

Of course, not every game you want is likely to be available in every casino you walk into. And sometimes you may locate your game of choice only to find that another player is seated at the machine with no intention of leaving it in the near future. This is a simple fact of casino life. Just don't get discouraged and start playing a bad-paying game or one that is unfamiliar to you. Believe me when I say that you'll be far happier if you take the time to find the best games available—even if it means picking yourself up and driving to a new casino. (See Chapter 5 for advice on locating the best video poker machines.)

Finally, remember that you won't know whether you've found the game you want until you compare pay tables. I'm sure you understand by now that not all Jacks or Better games offer good returns, and not all Deuces Wild games are the same. Carry your pay charts with you, and compare them to the pay tables found on the machines. When you find a match, you'll know for sure that you've located your game of choice.

Do you love the dramatic ups and downs of a game with high volatility? If so, there are several good games which can provide that adrenaline rush. Just don't be so focused on fun that you pick a poor-paying game or one that you don't know how to play.

PROGRESSIVE GAMES

No chapter on strategy would be complete without a discussion of progressive games. Why? Because finding and playing a progressive game is one of the best strategies you can use.

In *progressive games,* several video poker machines are linked together, and a portion of each bet made at any of these machines is designated to feed a common jackpot. The pot keeps growing as more money is made by the house until someone playing at one of the linked machines gets a specific winning hand—usually a Royal Flush, but sometimes a lesser hand such as Four of a Kind or a Straight Flush. The player then wins the entire jackpot, and the progressive jackpot is reset to a starting value.

The most important thing to remember about a progressive game is that *you must play the maximum number of coins to be eligible for the progressive jackpot.* Be aware that when you make a *short-coin bet*—a bet of less than maximum coins—you will be contributing to the jackpot, but will be ineligible to win it. I once witnessed a player who was betting 4 coins instead of the maximum 5 coins on a dollar progressive. After making his $4 wager, he drew a Royal Flush and received $1,000 (250 x 4 = 1,000) instead of the jackpot of over $8,500 he would have won if he had bet maximum coins. By saving *one dollar,* he lost over $7,500!

Even if you've never been to a casino, you'll find these machines easy to identify on your first visit, as they're usually arranged in a carousel above which a progressive meter shows the amount of the current jackpot.

Approximating the Expected Return of a Progressive Jackpot

When opportunity knocks in the form of a progressive jackpot, you'll want to open the door. You may, however, first want to do a few quick calculations to determine how the progressive will affect the expected return (ER) of the game. As you may already know, players are not allowed to use calculators or other electronic devices in a casino. Fortunately, you'll need just a pencil and paper to do the following calculations. You may even be able to do them in your head.

As explained earlier, most of the progressives are for the highest hand, which is the Royal Flush, and most require that you play maximum coins—usually, 5 coins. Both of the following methods of determining revised ERs assume that the Royal Flush pays 4,000 coins at reset—in other words, *without* the progressive. Both rules of thumb work for machines of all denominations.

Rule of Thumb One for Progressive Royals

This Rule of Thumb simply adds 1% to the game's regular (nonprogressive) ER for every 2,000 coins the Royal Flush pays above the 4,000-coin reset. I use this method to approximate the ER for progressives that are much higher than the reset value of 4,000 coins. Here are its four simple steps:

1. Determine the number of *coins (not dollars)* the jackpot is paying for the Royal Flush.

2. Determine the number of coins the jackpot is paying *above* the number of coins provided in the regular payout.

3. Divide the result of Step 2 by 2,000.

4. Multiply the result of Step 3 by 1%, and add that figure to the game's usual ER to approximate the new ER.

Let's look at a specific example. You choose to play 9/6 Jacks or Better, which has the following pay chart and ER for 5 coins:

5-10-15-20-30-45-125-250-4000 . . . 99.54%

As you can see from the pay chart, the regular Royal Flush pays 4,000 coins. The progressive jackpot, however, is paying $1,600 on a $.25 machine. Now, let's apply our system:

1. The progressive jackpot is paying $1,600. Because it's a $.25 machine, and there are four quarters to a dollar, this is equivalent to 6,400 coins. (1,600 x 4 = 6,400)

2. The progressive is paying 2,400 coins above the regular payout of 4,000 coins. (6,400 – 4,000 = 2,400).

3. You divide 2,400 by 2,000, and get 1.2.

4. When you multiply the figure from Step 3 by 1%, you get 1.2%. You add 1.2% to the game's usual ER of 99.54%, and find that the ER for the progressive game is approximately 100.74%.

It's not uncommon to find a progressive jackpot for 9/6 Jacks or Better, which is great news. Because of its ER, 9/6 Jacks or Better can be found even in casinos whose states mandate ERs lower than 100%. (You'll learn about state mandates in Chapter 5.) And with the progressive jackpot, the 9/6 Jacks or Better becomes a player advantage game.

Rule of Thumb Two for Progressive Royals

This second Rule of Thumb adds 0.1% to the game's usual ER for every 200 coins the Royal Flush pays above the 4,000-coin reset. I use this method to approximate the ER when the progressive is close to the reset value. Then, as I play the game, I mentally add 0.1% to the previous ER every time the progressive grows by 200 coins. Here are the steps:

1. Determine the number of *coins (not dollars)* the jackpot is paying for the Royal Flush.

2. Determine the number of coins the jackpot is paying *above* the number of coins provided in the regular payout.

3. Divide the result of Step 2 by 200.

4. Multiply the result of Step 3 by 0.1 percent, and add that figure to the game's usual ER to approximate the new ER.

Let's apply this formula to a particular example. Let's say that you choose to play 10/7 Double Bonus Poker, which has the following pay chart for 5 coins:

   5-5-15-25-35-50-250-400-800-250-4000 . . . 100.17%

As you can see, the regular Royal Flush pays 4,000 coins. The progressive jackpot, though, is paying $4,800 on a $1 machine. Let's apply the new formula:

1. The progressive jackpot is paying $4,800. Because it's a $1 machine, this is equivalent to 4,800 coins.

2. The progressive is paying 800 coins above the regular payout of 4,000 coins. (4,800 − 4,000 = 800)

3. You divide 800 by 200 and get 4.

4. You multiply the figure from Step 3 by 0.1% and get 0.4 %. (4 x 0.1% = 0.4%) You add 0.4% to the game's usual ER of 100.17%, and find that the ER for the progressive is approximately 100.57%.

In the above example, a good game—a player advantage game— becomes even better because of the bonus coins added by the progres-

Penalty Cards

If you've been talking to experienced players or reading some of the material now available on the game of video poker, you may have encountered the term *penalty cards*. What are these cards and should they affect your strategy? Let's address each of these questions in turn.

Penalty cards are defined as cards that if discarded will reduce your chance of drawing a Flush or a Straight. Note that the removal of these cards is necessary if you are to draw the primary target hands, but that this removal does reduce the chance of a secondary Straight or Flush payoff. Confused? A brief example should help you understand the concept.

Suppose you are dealt the following hand: the King of Hearts, Queen of Hearts, Jack of Hearts, Nine of Diamonds, and Seven of Hearts. You decide to keep the King, Queen, and Jack, hoping for a Royal Flush. If you discard the Nine and Seven—as you must, in order to attempt the Royal Flush—the absence of the Nine will reduce the chance of drawing a Straight. For this reason, the Nine is called a Straight Penalty. The absence of the Seven will reduce the chance of drawing a Flush. For this reason, the Seven is called a Flush Penalty.

Now let's address the second question posed above: Should penalty cards affect your strategy? Be aware that even experts argue over the value of the penalty card because this is such a complex subject. Some penalty card situations, however, have a greater impact on the game's ER than others. Experts do agree on one thing, though: It is far easier to learn and apply a strategy when you don't consider *every* penalty card situation. My strategy cards cover penalty card situations for frequent hands, since these hands would have a greater impact on the game's ER. So by using the strategy cards presented in the back of this book, you will enjoy video poker success and will learn to pay attention to only those penalty situations that really count.

sive. If you keep the above Rules of Thumb in mind, you'll be able to easily calculate a progressive game's ER both before you choose a game and as you play it—without drawing attention to yourself.

USING PLAYING STRATEGIES

You now know why some games are wiser choices than others, and you know how to identify the best-paying games available. You also understand how progressive jackpots can increase the value of a game, and you've learned why it's smart to always bet a maximum number of coins. Already, you have an advantage over many of the players you're likely to see in casinos. But as you know, there's more to playing video

Glossary of Useful Poker Terms

In Chapter 1, you learned the names of the different winning card combinations, such as Three of a Kind, Straight, and Royal Flush. But in the strategy tables offered on pages 70 to 81, you may find a few terms you don't know—especially if you're new to poker. Note that many of these terms are used not only in my strategy tables and cards, but throughout the worlds of both table poker and video poker. Learn what they mean, and you'll be more comfortable when playing in the casinos.

Consecutive Cards. A sequence of cards with no gaps or spaces between them. For example, a Seven, Eight, and Nine are three consecutive cards.

Four Flush. Four cards of the same suit—such as a Two of Hearts, Five of Hearts, Seven of Hearts, and Jack of Hearts—that need an additional card of that suit to make a Flush.

Gap. A space between cards that must be filled in order to make a consecutive sequence. For example, a Seven and a Ten have two gaps between them that must be filled by an Eight and Nine to make the cards consecutive.

High Cards. In most games, the Ace, King, Queen, and Jack. In Pick 'Em Poker, though, the high cards also include Nine and Ten.

High Pair. A paying pair for a particular game.

Inside Four-Straight. A broken sequence of four cards—such as Three, Five, Six, and Seven—that requires exactly one card (in this case, a Four) to make a Straight.

Low Cards. In most games, the number cards—Two, Three, Four, Five, Six, Seven, Eight, Nine, and Ten. In Pick 'Em Poker, though, Nine and Ten are considered high cards.

Low Pair. A nonpaying pair for a particular game.

Open-Ended Four-Straight. Four consecutive cards—such as Three, Four, Five, and Six—that need either one of two cards (in this case, a Two or a Seven) to make a Straight.

poker than comparing pay tables, choosing games, and betting the right number of coins. When you finally sit down at the machine, you have to know how to play the game.

True, there is an element of chance in the game of video poker. No matter what anyone may tell you, you can have no influence over the cards that are dealt to you. The only portion of the game that involves skill comes after the deal, when you decide which cards you will hold. The person who believes that common sense is all he needs to make this decision is destined to lose over the long run, because many correct holds are counterintuitive—they don't *seem* right, even though they are.

The serious player, on the other hand, trusts in a proven strategy that's the result of statistical analysis, and makes the best play most of the time.

Unfortunately, there's no one strategy that works for every video poker game. Each game—and each *version* of the same game—requires its own strategy. The good news is that you don't have to know the strategies for hundreds of different games to get the winning edge in video poker. You have to know the strategies for only a few games—the best games with the best payoffs.

For each dealt hand, the strategy tables presented in this chapter tell you exactly which cards you should hold, and also list exceptions and taboos. However, these tables, which are relatively detailed, are not appropriate for use in a noisy, chaotic casino. Furthermore, you won't want to draw a lot of attention to yourself by poring over game strategies while at the machine. That's why you'll want to use the tables in this chapter only for home practice. Then, when you finally enter a casino, you'll find the strategy cards at the back of the book more helpful.

Using the Home Study Strategy Tables

The following strategy tables are perfect for home study and practice, and will get you ready to use the more concise, condensed strategy cards in the back of the book. Just like the cards, each of the tables is the based on statistical analysis, and has been proven accurate time and time again in actual casino play.

Note that in each table, possible hand combinations are placed in order, with the highest-ranking hand at the top of the table. When using these tables, *always start at the top of the table and read downwards until you find the hand you were dealt.* This will ensure that you follow the directions for the highest-ranking combination in your hand.

Column 1 of each table describes various dealt hands, as just explained. Column 2 tells you which cards, if any, you should hold. Once you've located your hand, you should follow the instructions in Column 2 *unless* one of the exceptions provided in Column 3 applies to your situation. In that case, follow the instructions in Column 3, being aware that the exceptions are ranked by number in order of importance. In other words, if number 1 applies to your hand, follow it. If not, move on to number 2, etc. Finally, Column 4 lists taboos—actions you should

When using either the strategy tables found in this chapter or the strategy cards found in the back of the book, *always read from top to bottom.* This will ensure that you follow the proper directions for the hand you're holding.

never take when you've been dealt that particular hand. Don't ignore this column, as it can help you avoid major, expensive mistakes—mistakes that I've actually seen players make.

In most cases, the following tables are self-explanatory. But when penalty cards are involved, things get a bit more complex. If you want to take penalty cards into account, be sure to read the inset on page 67 and to learn the strategies. If penalty cards are more than you want to handle right now, feel free to ignore them while learning more basic strategies. You will still do well.

If you're relatively new to video poker and aren't sure of the hierarchy of hands in the various games whose strategies are provided below, turn back to Chapter 1, which presents the hierarchy of hands for each of these games. If you're a newcomer to poker and are unfamiliar with terms like Four Flush, turn to the inset on page 68. Finally, it pays to repeat that if you want to gain the winning edge in video poker, you have to first practice at home and become proficient at using these strategies. To learn about effective practice tools, see page 80.

**Table 3.14. Strategies for 9/6 Jacks or Better (99.54% ER),
9/6 Bonus Poker Deluxe (99.64% ER), and 8/5 Bonus Poker (99.17% ER)**

Dealt Hand (What You Have)	Hold Cards (What to Do)	Exceptions	Taboos (What You Should *Never* Do)
Royal Flush	Hold Royal Flush.	No exceptions.	**1.** Never choose the Double Down option that may be offered.
Straight Flush	Hold Straight Flush.	No exceptions.	**1.** Never hold four to a Royal Flush over a Straight Flush. Hold the Straight Flush.
Four of a Kind	Hold Four of a Kind	No exceptions.	No taboos.
Full House	Hold Full House.	No exceptions.	**1.** Never hold three Aces over a Full House— not even when playing Bonus Poker Deluxe or Bonus Poker. Always hold the Full House. **2.** Never hold Three of Kind over a Full House—not even when playing Bonus Poker Deluxe. Always hold the Full House.
Flush	Hold Flush.	**1.** Hold four to a Royal Flush.	**1.** Never hold a Flush over four to a Royal Flush. Hold only four to a Royal.
Straight	Hold Straight.	**1.** Hold four to a Royal Flush.	**1.** Never hold a Straight over four to a Royal Flush. Hold only four to a Royal.
Three of a Kind	Hold Three of a Kind.	No exceptions.	No taboos.

Dealt Hand (What You Have)	Hold Cards (What to Do)	Exceptions	Taboos (What You Should *Never* Do)
Two Pair	Hold both Pair.	No exceptions.	1. Never hold a Pair of Aces, Twos, Threes, or Fours (or any Pair, for that matter) when dealt Two Pair—not even when playing one of the Bonus Poker games. Always hold the Two Pair.
Jacks or Better	Hold high Pair.	1. Hold four to a Royal Flush. 2. Hold four to a Straight Flush. 3. In progressive 9/6 Jacks or Better, hold three to a progressive Royal when Royal is paying over 4,780 coins without a Flush Penalty. If Flush Penalty, hold if Royal pays over 5,050 coins. 4. In progressive 9/6 Jacks or Better, with Ace-Ten-any card combination, hold three to a Royal when Royal is paying over 5,335 coins without a Flush Penalty. If Flush Penalty, hold if paying over 5,605 coins.	1. Never hold a high Pair over four to a Royal Flush. Hold only four to a Royal. 2. Never hold a high Pair over four to a Straight Flush. Hold only four to a Straight Flush. 3. Never hold a high Pair in a high-paying Jacks or Better progressive. If you hold three to a progressive Royal, and an Ace is not one of the three, hold three to a Royal if paying over 4,780 coins without a Flush Penalty, or over 5,050 with a Flush Penalty. If an Ace *is* one of the three, hold three to a progressive Royal if paying over 5,335 coins without a Flush Penalty, or over 5,605 coins with a Flush Penalty
Four Flush	Hold Four Flush.	1. Hold three to a Royal Flush.	1. Never hold a Four Flush over three to a Royal Flush. Hold only the three to a Royal.
Low Pair	Hold the Pair.	1. Hold three to a Royal Flush.	1. Never hold a low Pair over three to a Royal Flush. Hold three to a Royal.
Open-Ended Four-Straight	Hold Four-Straight.	1. Hold three to a Royal Flush.	1. Never hold Open-Ended Four-Straight over three to a Royal Flush. Hold only three to a Royal.
Inside Four-Straight	Hold nothing.	1. Hold Inside Four-Straight with three or four high cards.	1. Never discard an Inside Four-Straight with three or four high cards. Hold the four cards.
High Cards	Hold high cards.	1. Hold three to a Royal Flush. 2. Hold two to a Royal Flush, unless Ace and Ten, King and Ten, or Queen and Ten. Then hold high cards. 3. When dealt three high cards, including an Ace, hold the two non-Ace high cards. 4. Hold three to any 0-gap or one-gap Straight Flush.	1. Never hold high cards over three to a Royal Flush. Hold three to a Royal. 2. Never hold suited Ace and Ten, King and Ten, or Queen and Ten to go for a Royal. Hold the high cards. (This assumes no progressive Royal.) 3. Never hold an Ace when dealt three high cards. Hold the two non-Ace high cards. 4. Never hold high cards when dealt three to a 0-gap or one-gap Straight Flush. Hold the cards to the Straight Flush.
No Pairs or High Cards	Hold nothing.	1. Hold three to a Straight Flush.	1. Never discard three to a Straight Flush. 2. Never hold three to a Straight or three to a Flush.

Table 3.15. **Strategies for Not-So-Ugly Deuces Wild (99.73% ER)**

Dealt Hand (What You Have)	Hold Cards (What to Do)	Exceptions	Taboos (What You Should *Never* Do)
Natural Royal Flush	Hold a Natural Royal Flush—a Royal Flush with no Deuces.	No exceptions.	1. Never choose the Double Down option that may be offered.
Wild Royal Flush	Hold Wild Royal Flush—a Royal Flush with one, two, or three Deuces.	1. When playing progressive Not-So-Ugly Deuces Wild paying more than 5,365 coins, if you have one Deuce, discard the Deuce and hold four to a Natural Royal Flush.	1. Never hold three Deuces instead of the Wild Royal. Hold the Wild Royal. (Note that this strategy is different for certain other Deuces wild games.) 2. Unless playing a progressive paying more than 5,365 coins, never hold four to the Royal instead of the Wild Royal. Hold the Wild Royal.
Four Deuces	Hold Four Deuces.	No exceptions.	No taboos.
Five of a Kind	Hold Five of a Kind.	No exceptions.	1. Never hold Three Deuces over Five of a Kind. Always hold Five of a Kind.
Straight Flush	Hold Straight Flush.	1. Hold three Deuces.	1. Never hold a Straight Flush over three Deuces. Hold just the three Deuces.
Four of a Kind	Hold Four of a Kind.	1. Hold three Deuces.	1. Never hold Four of a Kind over three Deuces. Hold the three Deuces.
Full House	Hold Full House.	No exceptions.	No taboos.
Flush	Hold Flush.	1. Hold four to a Royal Flush or four to a Wild Royal Flush. 2. Hold four to a Straight Flush if they include two Deuces and two cards Four and higher, with 0 gaps; or two Deuces and two cards Five and higher, with one gap. 3. Hold two Deuces.	1. Never hold a Flush over four to a Royal Flush. Hold just four to Royal Flush. 2. Never hold a Flush over four to a Straight Flush with two Deuces, two cards Four and Higher, 0 gaps; or two Deuces, two cards Five and higher, one gap. Hold the four cards. 3. Never hold a Flush over two Deuces. Hold just the Deuces.
Straight	Hold Straight.	1. Hold four to a Royal Flush. 2. Hold four to a Straight Flush if they include two Deuces and two cards Four and higher, with 0 gaps; or two Deuces and two cards Five and higher, with one gap. 3. Hold two Deuces.	1. Never hold a Straight over four to a Royal Flush. Hold just four to Royal Flush. 2. Never hold a Straight over four to a Straight Flush with two Deuces, two cards Four and Higher, 0 gaps; or two Deuces, two cards Five and higher, one gap. Hold the four cards. 3. Never hold a Straight over two Deuces. Hold just the Deuces.
Three of a Kind	Hold Three of a Kind.	1. Hold four to a Wild Royal Flush. 2. Hold four to a Straight Flush if they include two Deuces and two cards with 0 gaps, Four and higher (such as a Four and Five of Hearts); or Five and higher with one gap (such as Five and Seven of Hearts). 3. Hold two Deuces. 4. Hold four to a Straight Flush with one Deuce.	1. Never hold Three of a Kind over four to a Wild Royal Flush. Hold four to a Wild Royal. 2. Never hold Three of a Kind over four to a 0-gap Straight Flush with two Deuces, Four and higher; or Five and higher with one gap. Hold four to the Straight Flush. 3. Never hold Three of a Kind over two Deuces. Hold just the two Deuces. 4. Never hold one Deuce over four to a Straight Flush. Hold four to the Straight Flush.

Dealt Hand (What You Have)	Hold Cards (What to Do)	Exceptions	Taboos (What You Should Never Do)
Two Pair	Hold Two Pair.	1. Hold three to a Royal Flush.	1. Never hold Two Pair over three to a Royal Flush. Hold three to a Royal. 2. Never hold a Pair when dealt Two Pair. Hold both Pair.
One Pair (0 Deuces)	Hold Pair.	1. Hold three to a Royal Flush. 2. Hold Four Flush.	1. Never hold a Pair over three to a Royal Flush. Hold three to a Royal. 2. Never hold a Pair over a Four Flush. Hold the Four Flush.
Four Flush	Hold Four Flush.	1. Hold four to a Straight Flush with one Deuce. 2. Hold three to a Wild Royal or Natural Royal Flush. 3. Hold three to a Straight Flush if they include one Deuce and two cards Four and higher, with 0 gaps; or one Deuce and two cards Five and higher, with one gap. 4. Hold one Deuce.	1. Never hold a Four Flush over three to a Wild or Natural Royal Flush. Hold three to a Royal. 2. Never hold a Four Flush over three to a Straight Flush with one Deuce, two cards Four and higher, 0 gaps; or one Deuce, two cards Five and higher, one gap. Hold three to Straight Flush. 3. Never hold a Four Flush over one Deuce. Hold only the Deuce. 4. Never discard a Natural Four Flush—one with no Deuces. Hold the Natural Four Flush.
Open-Ended Four-Straight	Hold Open-Ended Four-Straight.	1. Hold three to a Wild Royal Flush or three to a Natural Royal. 2. Hold three to a Straight Flush if they include one Deuce and two cards Four and higher, with 0 gaps; or one Deuce and two cards Five and higher, with one gap. 3. Hold one Deuce—unless you have a Deuce plus unsuited Six, Seven, Eight; Seven, Eight, Nine; Eight, Nine, Ten; or Nine, Ten, Jack. Then, hold the four-card combo.	1. Never hold four to a Straight over three to a Wild or Natural Royal Flush. Hold three to a Royal. 2. Never hold four to a Straight over three to a Straight Flush with one Deuce, two cards Four and higher, 0 gaps; or one Deuce, two cards Five and higher, one gap. Hold three to Straight Flush. 3. Never hold four to a Straight with a Deuce. Hold just the Deuce. The exceptions are a Deuce plus unsuited Six, Seven, Eight; Seven, Eight, Nine; Eight, Nine, Ten; or Nine, Ten, Jack. Hold the four-card combo.
Inside Four-Straight	Hold Inside Four-Straight.	1. Hold three to a Wild Royal Flush or three to a Natural Royal. 2. Hold three to a Straight Flush if they include one Deuce and two cards Four and higher, with 0 gaps; or one Deuce and two cards Five and higher, with one gap. 3. Hold three to a Straight Flush with no Deuces. 4. Hold one Deuce. 5. Hold suited Jack and Ten, Jack and Queen, or Queen and Ten. 6. If the Inside Four-Straight includes an unsuited Ace, Three, Four, and Five, hold nothing.	1. Never hold four to a Straight over three to a Wild or Natural Royal Flush. Hold three to a Royal. 2. Never hold four to a Straight over three to a Straight Flush with one Deuce, two cards Four and higher, 0 gaps; or one Deuce, two cards Five and higher, one gap. Hold three to Straight Flush. 3. Never hold Inside Four-Straight over three to a Straight Flush with no Deuces. Hold three to Straight Flush. 4. Never hold Inside Four-Straight over one Deuce. Hold just the Deuce 5. Never hold an Inside Four-Straight over a suited Jack and Ten, Jack and Queen, or Queen and Ten. Hold the two cards. 6. Never hold an unsuited Ace, Three, Four, and Five. Hold nothing.

Dealt Hand (What You Have)	Hold Cards (What to Do)	Exceptions	Taboos (What You Should *Never* Do)
Three to Straight Flush (0 Deuces)	Hold three to a Natural Straight Flush—a Straight Flush with no Deuces.	No exceptions.	No taboos.
Three to Straight Flush (one Deuce)	Hold one Deuce.	1. Hold three to a Wild Royal Flush with one Deuce. 2. Hold three to a Straight Flush if they include one Deuce and two cards Four and higher, with 0 gaps; or one Deuce and two cards Five and higher, with one gap.	1. Never discard three to a Wild Royal with one Deuce. Hold three to Wild Royal. 2. Never throw away three to a 0-gap Straight Flush with one Deuce, Four and higher; or Five and higher with one gap. Hold three to Straight Flush.
High Cards	Hold nothing.	1. Hold three to a Royal Flush. 2. Hold two to a Royal unless one is an Ace. Then, hold nothing. 3. Hold one Deuce.	1. Never hold two or three unrelated high cards. In this case, hold nothing. 2. Never discard three to a Royal Flush. 3. Never hold two to a Royal if one is an Ace. Hold nothing. 4. Never discard a Deuce.

Table 3.16. **Strategies for Full-Pay Deuces Wild (100.76% ER)**

Dealt Hand (What You Have)	Hold Cards (What to Do)	Exceptions	Taboos (What You Should *Never* Do)
Natural Royal Flush	Hold a Natural Royal Flush (no Deuces).	No exceptions.	1. Never choose the Double Down option that may be offered.
Wild Royal Flush	Hold Wild Royal Flush (one, two, or three Deuces).	1. When playing progressive Full-Pay Deuces Wild paying *more* than 5,400 coins, if you have one Deuce, discard the Deuce and hold four to a Natural Royal Flush.	1. Never hold three Deuces instead of the Wild Royal. Hold the Wild Royal. 2. Unless playing a progressive paying more than 5,400 coins, never hold four to a Natural Royal instead of the Wild Royal. Hold the Wild Royal.
Four Deuces	Hold Four Deuces.	No exceptions.	No taboos.
Five of a Kind	Hold Five of a Kind.	1. Hold three Deuces instead of five Threes, Fours, Fives, Sixes, Sevens, Eights, or Nines.	1. Never hold five Threes, Fours, Fives, Sixes, Sevens, Eights, or Nines with three dealt Deuces. Hold just the Deuces.
Straight Flush	Hold Straight Flush.	1. Hold three Deuces.	1. Never hold a Straight Flush when dealt three Deuces. Hold just the Deuces.
Four of a Kind	Hold Four of a Kind.	1. Hold three Deuces.	1. Never hold Four of a Kind when dealt three Deuces. Hold just the Deuces.
Full House	Hold Full House.	No exceptions.	No taboos.
Flush	Hold Flush.	1. Hold four to a Natural Royal Flush or four to a Wild Royal Flush. 2. Hold four to a Straight Flush if they include two Deuces and two cards Six and higher, with 0 gaps. 3. Hold two Deuces.	1. Never hold a Flush over four to a Natural or Wild Royal. Hold just the four to a Royal. 2. Never hold a Flush over four to a Straight Flush with two Deuces, two cards Six and higher, 0 gaps. Hold just the four cards. 3. Never hold a Flush when dealt two Deuces. Hold just the Deuces.

Dealt Hand (What You Have)	Hold Cards (What to Do)	Exceptions	Taboos (What You Should *Never* Do)
Straight	Hold Straight.	**1.** Hold four to a Natural Royal Flush or four to a Wild Royal Flush. **2.** Hold four to a Straight Flush if they include two Deuces and two cards Six and higher, with 0 gaps. **3.** Hold two Deuces.	**1.** Never hold a Straight over four to a Natural or Wild Royal Flush. Hold just the four to Royal Flush. **2.** Never hold a Straight over four to a Straight Flush with two Deuces, two cards Six and higher, 0 gaps. Hold just the four cards. **3.** Never hold a Straight when dealt two Deuces. Hold just the Deuces.
Three of a Kind	Hold Three of a Kind.	**1.** Hold four to a Wild Royal Flush. **2.** Hold four to a Straight Flush if they include two Deuces and two cards Six and higher, with 0 gaps. **3.** Hold two Deuces. **4.** Hold four to a Straight Flush if they include one Deuce and three cards Five and higher, with 0 gaps.	**1.** Never hold Three of a Kind over four to a Wild Royal. Hold four to Wild Royal. **2.** Never hold Three of a Kind over four to a Straight Flush with two Deuces, two cards Six and higher, 0 gaps. Hold four to the Straight Flush. **3.** Never hold Three of a Kind when dealt two Deuces. Hold just the Deuces. **4.** Never hold Three of a Kind over four to a Straight Flush with one Deuce, three cards Five and higher, and 0 gaps. Hold four to the Straight Flush.
Two Pair	Hold one Pair.	**1.** Hold three to a Royal Flush.	**1.** Never hold one Pair over three to a Royal Flush. Hold three to a Royal. **2.** Never hold both Pair when dealt Two Pair. Hold only one Pair.
One Pair (0 Deuces)	Hold Pair.	**1.** Hold three to a Royal Flush.	**1.** Never hold Pair over three to a Royal Flush. Hold three to a Royal.
Four Flush	Hold Four Flush.	**1.** Hold three to a Natural Royal Flush. **2.** Hold three to a Wild Royal, unless one is an Ace. Then hold just the Deuce. **3.** Hold three to a Straight Flush if they include one Deuce, two cards Six and higher, and 0 gaps. **4.** Hold one Deuce.	**1.** Never hold four to a Flush over three to a Natural Royal Flush. Hold three to a Royal Flush. **2.** Never hold three to a Wild Royal if one card is an Ace. Hold just the Deuce. **3.** Never hold a Four Flush over three to a Straight Flush with one Deuce, two cards Six and higher, 0 gaps. **4.** Never hold a Four Flush with one Deuce. Hold just the Deuce.
Four Straight (Open-Ended or Inside)	Hold four to a Straight.	**1.** Hold three to a Natural Royal Flush. **2.** Hold three to a Wild Royal unless one is an Ace. Then, hold just the Deuce. **3.** Hold three to a Straight Flush if they include one Deuce, two cards Six and higher, and 0 gaps. **4.** Hold one Deuce. **5.** If an Inside Four-Straight includes an unsuited Ace, Three, Four, and Five, hold nothing.	**1.** Never hold four to a Straight over three to a Natural Royal Flush. Hold three to a Royal. **2.** Never hold three to a Wild Royal if one card is an Ace. Hold just the Deuce. **3.** Never hold four to a Straight over three to a Straight Flush with one Deuce, two cards Six and higher, 0 gaps. **4.** Never hold a Four Straight with one Deuce. Hold just the Deuce. **5.** Never hold an unsuited Ace, Three, Four, and Five to a Straight. Hold nothing.

Dealt Hand (What You Have)	Hold Cards (What to Do)	Exceptions	Taboos (What You Should *Never* Do)
Three to Straight Flush (0 Deuces)	Hold three to Straight Flush.	1. Do not hold three to a Straight Flush if the Ace is a low card.	1. Never hold three to a Straight Flush if the Ace is a low card. In that case, hold nothing.
Three to Straight Flush (one Deuce)	Hold one Deuce.	1. Hold three to a Wild Royal Flush unless one card is an Ace and there is either a Straight or Flush Penalty. Then, hold just the Deuce. 2. Hold three to a Straight Flush if it includes one Deuce, two cards Six and higher, and 0 gaps.	1. Never hold three to a Wild Royal if one card is an Ace and there is a Straight or Flush Penalty. Then, hold just the Deuce. 2. Never hold just a Deuce over three to a Straight Flush with one Deuce, two cards Six and higher, 0 gaps. Hold three to Straight Flush.
High Cards	Hold nothing.	1. Hold three to a Royal Flush. 2. Hold two to a Royal Flush unless one card is an Ace. Then, hold nothing. 3. Hold two to a Royal Flush unless either card has a Straight or Flush Penalty. Penalty cards do not apply to Jack and Ten, Queen and Jack, or Queen and Ten combinations. If penalty cards, hold nothing. 4. Hold one Deuce.	1. Never discard three to a Royal. 2. Never hold two to a Royal if one card is an Ace. Hold nothing. 3. Never discard a Deuce.

Table 3.17. **Strategies for 10/7 Double Bonus Poker (100.17% ER)**

Dealt Hand (What You Have)	Hold Cards (What to Do)	Exceptions	Taboos (What You Should *Never* Do)
Royal Flush	Hold Royal Flush.	No exceptions.	1. Never choose the Double Down option that may be offered.
Straight Flush	Hold Straight Flush.	No exceptions.	1. Never discard a Straight Flush to go for a Royal Flush. Hold all cards.
Four of a Kind	Hold Four of a Kind.	No exceptions.	No taboos.
Full House	Hold Full House.	1. Hold three Aces.	1. Never hold a Full House over three Aces. Hold the Aces only.
Flush	Hold Flush.	1. Hold four to a Royal Flush.	1. Never hold a Flush over four to a Royal Flush. Hold four to a Royal only.
Straight	Hold Straight.	1. Hold four to a Royal Flush.	1. Never hold a Straight over four to a Royal Flush. Hold four to a Royal only.
Three of a Kind	Hold Three of a Kind.	No exceptions.	No taboos.
Two Pair	Hold both Pair.	No exceptions.	1. Never hold two Aces over Two Pair. Hold the Two Pair.

Dealt Hand (What You Have)	Hold Cards (What to Do)	Exceptions	Taboos (What You Should *Never* Do)
Jacks or Better	Hold high Pair.	**1.** Hold four to a Royal Flush. **2.** Hold four to a Straight Flush. **3.** Hold suited Ten, Jack, Queen; or suited Jack, Queen, King, unless Pair of Aces. If you have a Pair of Aces, hold the Aces.	**1.** Never hold Jacks or Better over four to a Royal Flush. Always hold four to the Royal Flush. **2.** Never hold Jacks or Better over four to a Straight Flush. Hold four to the Straight Flush. **3.** Never hold Jacks or Better over suited Ten, Jack, Queen; or suited Jack, Queen, King, unless Pair of Aces. In that case, hold only the Aces
Four Flush	Hold Four Flush.	**1.** Hold a suited Ten, Jack, and Queen to a Royal Flush.	**1.** Never hold a Four Flush over a suited Ten, Jack, and Queen to Royal Flush. Hold Ten, Jack, and Queen to the Royal Flush.
Open-Ended Four-Straight	Hold four to Straight.	**1.** Hold three to a Royal Flush.	**1.** Never hold four to a Straight over three to a Royal Flush. Hold three to any Royal Flush.
Low Pair	Hold the Pair.	**1.** Hold three to a Royal Flush.	**1.** Never hold a low (nonpaying) Pair over three to a Royal Flush. Hold three to any Royal.
High Cards	Hold high cards.	**1.** Hold three to a Royal Flush. **2.** Hold four to any Straight that includes two high cards. **3.** Hold unsuited Ten, Jack, and Queen instead of just unsuited Jack and Queen. **4.** Hold two to a Royal unless it's an Ace and Ten. Then, hold just the Ace. **5.** Hold three to any Flush if there are high cards in the three to a Flush, or three to any Straight Flush. **6.** If dealt an unsuited Ace and another high card, hold just the Ace if there is no Flush Penalty in the suit of the Ace. If there is a Flush Penalty, hold both high cards.	**1.** Never hold high cards over three to any Royal. Hold three to a Royal. **2.** Never hold just high cards if dealt four to any Straight that includes two high cards. Hold four to a Straight. **3.** Never hold just an unsuited Jack and Queen if also dealt a Ten. Hold three to the Straight. **4.** Never hold a suited Ace and Ten to a Royal Flush. Hold just the Ace. **5.** Never hold unrelated high cards over a three to a Flush that includes a high card. Hold three to the Flush. **6.** Never hold an unsuited high card and Ace if no Flush Penalty. Hold just the Ace.
Inside Four-Straight	Hold four to Inside Straight.	No exceptions.	No taboos.
Three to a Flush	Hold three to a flush.	No exceptions.	No taboos.

Table 3.18. **Strategies for 9/6 Double Double Bonus Poker (98.98% ER)**

Dealt Hand (What You Have)	Hold Cards (What to Do)	Exceptions	Taboos (What You Should *Never* Do)
Royal Flush	Hold Royal Flush.	No exceptions.	**1.** Never choose the Double Down option that may be offered.
Four of a Kind with a Kicker*	Hold all five cards.	No exceptions.	**1.** Never hold just the Four of a Kind without the kicker. Hold all five cards.
Four of a Kind with no Kicker	Hold Four of a Kind.	No exceptions.	**1.** Never hold all five cards. Hold just the Four of a Kind.
Four of a Kind, Fives through Kings	Hold all cards.	No exceptions.	No taboos.
Full House	Hold Full House.	**1.** Hold three Aces.	**1.** Never hold a Full House over three Aces. Hold just the three Aces. **2.** Never hold three Twos, Threes, or Fours over a Full House. Hold the Full House.
Flush	Hold Flush.	**1.** Hold four to a Royal Flush.	**1.** Never hold four to a Straight Flush over a Flush. Hold the Flush. **2.** Never hold a Flush over four to a Royal Flush. Hold four to a Royal.
Straight	Hold Straight.	**1.** Hold four to a Royal Flush.	**1.** Never hold a Straight over four to a Royal Flush. Hold just the four to a Royal. **2.** Never hold four to a Straight Flush over a Straight. Hold the Straight.
Three of a Kind	Hold Three of a Kind.	No exceptions.	No taboos.
Two Pair	Hold Two Pair.	**1.** Hold Pair of Aces.	**1.** Never hold Two Pair over Pair of Aces. Hold just the Aces. **2.** Never hold a Pair of Twos, Threes, or Fours over Two Pair. Hold both Pair.
Jacks or Better	Hold high Pair.	**1.** Hold four to a Royal Flush. **2.** Hold a suited Jack, Queen, and King, unless you have a Pair of Aces. In that case, hold the Aces. **3.** When playing six-way progressive Double Double Bonus Poker, hold three to a Royal when the Royal is worth 4,955 coins or more, unless Pair of Aces. (No Flush Penalty; must be 5,225 if Flush Penalty.) **4.** When playing six-way progressive Double Double Bonus Poker, hold three to a Royal when the Royal is	**1.** Never hold a high Pair over four to a Royal Flush. Hold four to a Royal. **2.** Never hold a high Pair over suited Jack, Queen, and King, unless it is a Pair of Aces. In that case, hold the Aces. **3.** Never hold a high Pair other than Aces over three to any Royal when the progressive is over 4,955 coins, and no Flush Penalty. (5,225 coins with Flush Penalty.) If Pair of Aces, hold three to Royal at 7,500 or more coins, no Flush Penalty. (Hold three to Royal over Pair of Aces at 7,800 or more coins, with

Dealt Hand (What You Have)	Hold Cards (What to Do)	Exceptions	Taboos (What You Should *Never* Do)
Jacks or Better *(continued)*		worth 7,500 coins or more, if Pair of Aces. (No Flush Penalty; must be 7,800 coins if Flush Penalty.)	Flush Penalty.)
Four Flush	Hold Four Flush.	**1.** Hold three to a Royal Flush.	**1.** Never hold a Four Flush over three to a Royal Flush. Hold three to a Royal.
Low Pair	Hold low Pair.	**1.** Hold Open-Ended Four-Straight with any high card.	**1.** Never hold a low Pair over an Open-Ended Four-Straight with one or more high cards. Hold four to the Straight.
Open-Ended Four-Straight	Hold Open-Ended Four-Straight.	**1.** Hold three to a Royal Flush.	**1.** Never hold an Open-Ended Four-Straight over three to a Royal Flush. Hold three to a Royal.
Three to Straight Flush	Hold three to Straight Flush.	**1.** Hold three to a Royal Flush. **2.** Hold three to a Straight Flush, Three and higher, with 0 gaps. **3.** Hold two high cards to a Royal Flush over three to a low card Straight Flush with gaps. **4.** Hold high cards over three to a low card Straight Flush with two gaps.	**1.** Never hold three to a low card Straight Flush with one or two gaps over two high cards to a Royal. Always hold two high cards to a Royal. **2.** Never hold three to a low card Straight Flush with gaps over three to a low card Straight Flush 0 gaps. Hold the cards with no gaps. **3.** Never hold three to a low card Straight Flush with gaps over two high cards to a Royal Flush. Hold two to a Royal. **4.** Never hold three to a low card Straight Flush with two gaps over miscellaneous high cards. Hold the high cards.
High Cards	Hold high cards.	**1.** Hold two cards to a Royal Flush unless Flush Penalty. With a Flush Penalty, hold four to an Ace-high straight. **2.** Hold four to a Straight with two or more high cards. **3.** Hold an Ace instead of two unsuited high cards. **4.** Hold an Ace instead of three unsuited high cards unless an Ace, Queen, and Jack. Then hold Queen and Jack. **5.** Hold a suited King and Ten, Queen and Ten, or Jack and Ten instead of one high card.	**1.** Never hold high cards over four to any Straight that includes two or more high cards. Hold four to the Straight. **2.** Never hold two unsuited high cards over an Ace. Hold just the Ace. **3.** Never hold an unsuited Ace, Queen, and Jack. Hold the Queen and Jack only. **4.** Never discard a suited King and Ten, Queen and Ten, or Jack and Ten.
Insight Four-Straight	Hold Inside Four-Straight.	No exceptions.	No taboos.

*In this game, a Kicker is an Ace, Two, Three, or Four.

Earlier in the chapter, you learned how the strategy tables are set up from page 70 to page 79. All of those tables are arranged in the same way because all of the games they cover are played in approximately the same way. (You are given five cards, and decide which, if any, you are going to hold.) As you learned in Chapter 1, though, Pick 'Em Poker is a very different game.

In Pick 'Em, you are dealt two unchangeable cards on the left, and you can "pick" from two stacks of cards on the right. Each of the stacks has three cards in it, but you are able to see only the top card. Based on those top cards—and, of course, on the two cards that you *must* hold—you choose one of the stacks to complete your hand. (For more information on Pick 'Em, see page 16 in Chapter 1.)

When using Table 3.19, the strategy table for Pick 'Em, start at the top and work your way to the bottom, just as you did when using the earlier strategy tables. You'll want to first look at Column 1, which shows you the card combination you will have *after* you have selected one of the two stacks. (For instance, when you see Three of a Kind in Column 1, it simply means that the two unchangeable cards and the card at the top of one stack makes Three of a Kind.) Column 2 lists situations in which you should not pick that stack, or helps you choose between two stacks when either one will give you the listed card combination. Finally, Column 3 presents taboos—actions you should never take in that situation.

Even a quick glance at Table 3.19 will show you that Pick 'Em involves fewer possible combinations than the other video poker games discussed in this book. But as you'll learn when you play the game, this element makes Pick 'Em fast and fun.

THE IMPORTANCE OF PRACTICE

While you might think that strategy cards or strategy tables alone will enable you to play a perfect or near-perfect game of video poker, unfortunately, it doesn't work that way. Before you can play accurately in a casino environment, you have to become accustomed to using the strategies presented in this book. Of course, practice is especially important for people who are not yet familiar with poker and its terms, and can't immediately recognize certain hands—an Inside Four-Straight, for instance. But even the experienced table poker player, who

Table 3.19. Strategies for Pick 'Em Poker (99.95% ER)

Dealt Hand With Top Card of Selected Stack	Exceptions and Alternatives	Taboos (What You Should Never Do)
Three of a Kind	No exceptions.	No taboos.
Three to a Royal Flush	1. If one of the three to a Royal Flush is an Ace, if possible, select the stack that makes a high Pair.	1. Never select a stack that makes three to a Royal Flush if one of the three is an Ace, over a high Pair. Always choose the high Pair.
High Pair (Paying Pair)	No exceptions.	1. Never select a stack that makes three to a Straight Flush over a high Pair. Always choose the high Pair.
Three to a Straight Flush (0 or One Gap)	1. If both stacks make three to a Straight Flush, select the stack with 0 gaps. 2. If the stacks have the same number of gaps, select the high card stack.	1. Never select the one-gap stack over the 0-gap stack when both stacks make three to a Straight Flush. Hold the 0-gap stack. 2. Never select the stack with an Eight or less over the stack with a Nine or higher if both stacks have the same number of gaps. Hold the high card stack.
Low Pair (Non-Paying Pair)	1. If one of the stacks is a high card and makes three to a two-gap Straight Flush, select it instead of the stack that makes a low Pair.	1. Never select a low Pair stack over a three to a Flush stack when two of the three cards are high. Select three to a Flush. 2. Never select a low Pair stack over three to a two-gap Straight Flush when any of the three cards is high. Hold the Straight Flush stack. 3. Never select a two-gap Straight Flush stack with three low cards. Select the low Pair stack.
Three to a Straight Flush (Two Gaps)	1. If both stacks make three to a Straight Flush with two gaps, select the high card stack.	No taboos.
Three to a Flush	1. If both stacks make three to a Flush, select the high card stack.	No taboos.
Three to a Straight (0 or One Gap)	1. If both stacks make three to a Straight with 0 or one gap, select the high card stack. 2. If both stacks have either high or low cards, select the stack with the fewest gaps.	1. Never select a low card stack with 0 gaps over a high card stack with one gap. Hold the high card stack. 2. Never select a one-gap stack over a 0-gap stack if the stacks are either both high or both low. Hold the 0-gap stack.
High Card (Nine or Higher)	1. If both stacks have high cards, select the stack that makes three to any Straight.	1. Never select a stack without a Straight possibility over a stack with a Straight possibility if both stacks have high cards. (Note that Nine is a high card in this game.)
Three to a Low Straight (Two Gaps)	No exceptions.	1. Never select a stack without a Straight possibility if nothing above applies. Hold the two-gap Straight stack.
Low Card	1. If both stacks are low and nothing above applies, select either card.	No taboos.

To hone your video poker skills, purchase and use a good computer tutorial program. These programs will enable you to practice your video poker strategies at home, without losing your bankroll.

knows a Straight from a Flush, has to learn the ins and outs of video poker play. That's why home practice is so important. Through use of a computer tutorial program, you can apply your strategies away from the noise and distractions of a busy casino, and without the threat of losing your bankroll. This will allow you to hone your skills until you can play quickly and accurately in any environment.

Fortunately, several different companies have created excellent tutorial programs for video poker. (See the Resource List on page 143.) Once you have purchased a tutorial program and installed it on your home computer, you'll be able to select a game, change the pay table, determine the expected return, play the game, analyze your errors, and much more. If you find an unusual new game in a casino, you will often be able to adjust your practice program to create the game you saw. You'll even be able to use special teaching modes that alert you to errors as you play, help you focus on difficult hands that have stumped you in the past, and permit you to adjust pay tables for video poker tournament play.

Too often, new video poker players grab their strategy cards and rush off to the nearest casino, only to lose their cash. Be smart, and take the time to practice until you have truly gained the winning edge in video poker.

MOVING ON

You are now ready to get the most out of your casino play. You know how to find the best games, and you have the tools you need to play those games correctly. But as you've learned, video poker is inherently volatile, with some games being more volatile than others. No matter how good your strategy may be, it is possible to win or lose quite a bit of money during any gambling session, especially if that session is only three or four hours long. Add to this the fact that the majority of new players underestimate the bankroll required to play at specific limits for a long period of time, and you'll understand the need for good money management skills. That's why Chapter 4 presents a solid money management program that will allow you to enjoy your time at the casino and stay within your budget.

MONEY
MANAGEMENT

Dan Paymar. Bob Dancer. Jean Scott. What do these people have in common? They are all expert video poker players. What else do they have in common? They are all experts in money management. Surprised? The fact is that knowing how to manage money is almost as important as knowing how to play the games, and is one of the factors that separates the losers from the winners. Experts, of course, use fairly sophisticated measures to determine their risk of losing their bankroll, called *risk of ruin*, or ROR. Dan Paymar, for example, uses the Sorokin Formula, while Bob Dancer makes sure he is bankrolled for three to five times the Royal Flush payout. Jean Scott would never play a denomination beyond either her financial means or what she calls her "psychological" level of comfort—and neither should you. Knowing how to manage money is an important skill when playing *any* casino game.

Fortunately, the principles of smart money management are not a secret. They are widely known, and although they do require some discipline, they are not difficult to follow. This chapter won't confound you with the Sorokin Formula or with any other complicated computations. Instead, it will fill you in on some simple and sound money management techniques that will allow your bankroll to last for your whole vacation, and, with some luck and skill, help you go home a winner.

DETERMINE YOUR BANKROLL AND STICK WITH IT

Creating a gambling budget and sticking to it, no matter how much you win or lose, is at the heart of proper money management. But it's not always as easy as it sounds. Under certain conditions, even the experienced gambler may be tempted to deviate from her plan and gamble just a little more, and then a little more . . . until her bankroll disappears. Are there concrete steps you can take to stay within your budget? Of course!

Establish Your Gambling Budget

Be sure to establish your gambling budget *before* you leave home, and to keep your gambling bankroll separate from the money you plan to spend on hotel accommodations, dining, and entertainment. This step is key to smart money management.

Clearly, your very first step—one you should take before you leave home—is to decide on the amount of your total gambling bankroll. As this amount will differ from individual to individual, I can't offer you guidance on choosing a sum, but I can tell you that this should be separate from your other money—from the money you will spend on your hotel accommodations and dining, for instance. I can also tell you that even if your gambling bankroll is sizeable, managing your money makes sense. Video poker is a fast-paced game, and—especially if you play high denomination and multi-hand machines—it's astoundingly easy to run through even a large bankroll in a short amount of time.

If you will be spending just a day at a casino, at this point, your course is pretty clear. You'll simply gamble up to the limits of your bankroll, and avoid betting even a penny beyond it. If, however, you will be spending two or more days at your gambling destination, it's a smart idea to take your total bankroll and divide it into session bankrolls. For the sake of simplicity, let's say that you have earmarked $1,000 as your gambling bankroll, and you are staying at the casino for five days. You will therefore have a $200 session bankroll for each day. If you plan to play two sessions a day—one in the afternoon and one in the evening, for instance—you can further divide each daily bankroll into two smaller ones of $100 each. To be sure that your money lasts for your whole vacation, it's helpful to place the cash for each session in a separate envelope, and mark it with the day and, if appropriate, with the time. For instance, an envelope might be allocated for "Saturday afternoon." Then take only the amount in the envelope with you to the casino for each session, leaving the rest in your hotel room. If you lose your bankroll, stop playing and find something else to do with your time. See the sights, enjoy a good meal, shop, or just relax. What if you win money? Some people immediately use their winnings for play, rationalizing that they're gambling with the casino's money. Always remember that once you win money, it's *yours*—not the casino's. And while there's no law against placing a wager with your winnings, consider the option of putting the cash in a safe place, far from the casino floor. Then, when you get home, you'll have a nice windfall.

Closely tied to the idea of choosing a gambling budget is that of choosing a time limit for each gambling session. It is my belief that—especially when you are learning the game—a two-hour session maximum is a good idea. Beyond this time, you may find it difficult to remain focused and make smart decisions.

If you're staying in a hotel, one last tip is in order. Instead of leaving your bankroll in the top drawer of your dresser, take advantage of the free safety deposit boxes that almost every casino and hotel now has to offer. This will help you enjoy your time at the casino without worrying about the safety of your cash and other valuables. Some players even say that the safety deposit box helps them stick to their budget. Whenever they're tempted to spend tomorrow's bankroll today, they have to go to their box to get their money. In the time it takes them to get from the casino to the safety deposit box and retrieve their cash, cooler reasoning often kicks in, and they leave their money where it is.

Stay Away From ATMs and Credit Cards

The game of video poker is exciting, and if you end up running through the money you've allotted for a session, you may be tempted to use your credit card or visit the nearest ATM just to stay in the action. Don't. As already discussed, it's important to stay within the boundaries you determined before you left home. If and when you lose a session bankroll, walk away from the casino and find something else to do until your next gambling session. If you're playing at a local casino, it's best to leave both credit and ATM cards at home. This will remove the temptation to play beyond your means. Finally, remember that you should be gambling with only the money you can afford to lose—not with your mortgage payment.

Avoiding ATMs not only makes good financial sense, but also increases enjoyment of the casino experience. Many players who make frequent trips to ATMs say that they are so stressed about going over their intended budget, they don't enjoy the game.

Avoid Moving to a Higher-Denomination Game to Recover Losses

Many players feel desperate when they find themselves losing their bankroll, and try to make up for losses by playing a higher denomination. This is a good way to lose even *more* money.

First, player advantage games are rarely found in higher denominations. This means that when you move up a denomination in an effort to recover losses, you will probably increase the likelihood of digging even deeper into your budget. Second, by now you should know the most important rule for minimizing your losses: *Never gamble more than what you set aside for that particular session.* If a session is not going your way—if you find yourself on a cold streak—the wisest action may be to quit and walk away. You can start again at your next session.

Know When to Quit

If sticking to your playing budget is the number-one principle of money management, the second most important rule is knowing when to walk away from the game. By now you understand that when you've lost all the money for a particular session, it's time to leave the casino and find another diversion. In fact, as mentioned above, it is often smart to walk away *before* you lose that session's bankroll. But what if you're winning? It is my belief that when you're on a winning streak, you should continue to play—but only until the end of your predetermined session time. If, for instance, you have decided to play for two hours, leave when those hours are up *even if you're ahead.* Playing beyond that time may lead to mistakes due to fatigue.

Keep in mind that some casinos actually pressure customers to keep playing in order to maintain their comp status. If you're familiar with casino play, you already know that upon entering a casino, you should apply for a slot club card, as continued use of it can win you cash and *comps*—complimentary service that may include meal vouchers at hotel restaurants, tickets to a show, or even a free room. (To learn more about this card, see page 91.) While I encourage you to obtain and use a slot club card—and to take advantage of all promotions that turn casino advantage games into player advantage games—years of experience have taught me that it's better to pay for your own room, food, and entertainment than to bust the bank for a comp. Don't let the casinos pressure you into playing when you're on a losing streak or, for that matter, when you're ahead, but have reached the end of your gambling session. There's nothing wrong with going home a winner.

CAREFULLY CHOOSE
BOTH YOUR CASINO AND YOUR GAMES

The techniques already described in this chapter will help you remain within the budget you have established. But there is more to money management than budgets and bankrolls. To get the most play from each of your session bankrolls, you'll want to wisely choose your casino and your games, and use intelligent strategies during each and every game you play.

You may already know that some casinos offer better-paying games than others, and that some, at various times, offer great promotions that can turn casino advantage games into player advantage games. This subject is explored more fully in Chapter 5, which also discusses the various types of casinos now in operation, and offers cautions about casinos that may not provide the regulated games you're looking for. I urge you to read that chapter fully. For the time being, be aware that it makes financial sense to learn some basic information about casinos, and—before going on your next gambling trip—to gather all the information you can about upcoming promotions.

In Chapter 3, I explained that to increase your odds of going home a winner, you'll want to compare the pay tables, expected returns, and volatility of the video poker games offered at any given casino. In fact, your budget may prohibit you from playing highly volatile games, because they often require large budgets. If you skipped over Chapter 3, please go back and read it carefully. Choosing a game on the basis of the factors just mentioned is essential if you are to get the most play for your bankroll. But the smart player is aware of other important factors as well. Let's look at some of them.

Choose Games That You Know

It sounds obvious, but because so many people ignore this fundamental rule, I feel I have to say it: *You must choose a video poker game that you*

If you find yourself on a losing streak, don't hesitate to leave the casino floor— even if you have part of your allocated bankroll left, and even if you planned to play longer. You can always resume play at another time.

know and have practiced at home. Remember that the expected return applies only when the game is played accurately, and accuracy is impossible when you aren't familiar with the game.

Many people wonder how casinos can offer video poker games that have 100% returns. Don't they lose money on these games? The fact is that the vast majority of players make many errors, basing their "strategy" on guesses or hunches. This reduces their achieved payback by 2 to 4%, enabling the casinos to make a profit in spite of a few good players.

The moral of the story is that you must understand and practice using the strategies for a specific game before you bet your money on it. (For information on video poker tutorial programs, see page 80.) And when you choose a game, it's vital to not only look at the name of the game, such as Deuces Wild, but to also match pay tables, as I instructed you to do in Chapter 3. Why? Unless you match pay tables, you won't know whether you've found the specific game you want—the version for which you have learned the playing strategies, and the one that offers the best expected return available.

A last thought: If you find that the casino you've chosen does not offer the favorable games that you know how to play, leave the casino and find one that has the games you want. Sometimes a casino will remove or downgrade certain games to reduce the player advantage. For instance, it might change 9/6 Jacks or Better to 9/5 Jacks or Better. Again, leave the casino, first letting the management know why you've chosen to take your business elsewhere.

Consider Moving Down a Denomination

When video poker made its debut in the mid-seventies, management kept upping the ante to attract more players. Finally, the casinos offered some games with payback percentages over 100%. As explained earlier in the chapter, they lost no money on these games because most people couldn't play them properly. Over time, though, more and more people learned effective playing strategies and were able to win fairly consistently. Management responded again, this time by no longer allowing the best-paying games in high-denomination machines.

What does this mean to you, a player who's trying to wisely manage her money? It means that if you find yourself on a losing streak but you still want to play, you can switch from dollars to quarters or from quarters to nickels. Not only will you then get more play out of every dollar you bet, but you'll probably also enjoy better returns.

I discourage playing less then the maximum number of coins because you then lose too much on the Royal Flush, which generally pays 800 to 1 with maximum coins, but only 250 to 1 with fewer than max coins. Keep in mind that it's mathematically wiser to play max coins in a small-denomination machine than it is to play short coins in a large-denomination machine. But if you insist on playing fewer than the maximum number of coins, it's better to play 1 coin than to play 4 in a 5-coin maximum machine. Simply put, you'll do less damage using this strategy.

Just as the casinos pressure people to keep playing to maintain comp status, they also pressure people to play higher denominations. If someone from the casino urges you to move from the nickel machine to the quarter or dollar machine, let him know that when the casino offers full-pay games in higher-denomination machines, you'll be glad to switch.

Don't Be Fooled by Deceptive Games

Above, you learned that it's often smart to move down a denomination—to switch from a dollar game to a quarter or nickel game, for instance. But when trying to play a low-denomination game, it's easy to fall into a common trap that can cause you to run through your bankroll very quickly.

These days, the fact is that many very low-denomination games are found on multi-hand machines. If you read Chapter 2, you may recall that these machines allow you to play from one to a hundred hands of the same game at the same time. (See the inset on page 30 to learn about multi-hand games.) This means that your wager is multiplied by the number of hands you play. Let's say, for instance, that you find a so-called penny game. If you bet maximum coins, which you should, you'll be paying a nickel per hand. And if you play 100 hands, your wager will be $5 a game—not a penny. While playing fewer hands may seem like a good option, be aware that this will result in a payback penalty. This doesn't mean that you should avoid multi-hand machines, but it does mean that you should be realistic about the amount of

If you decide to move down a denomination, check the pay table to make sure that the new machine provides an expected return that's as good as the ER of the machine you're leaving.

money you're wagering when choosing this casino option. You should also carefully examine the pay table before you play a multi-hand game, because it's rare to find a full-pay version of the games I recommend on these machines. Considering the money you'll be wagering, you certainly want to choose a good game.

The second deception is posed by Multistrike Poker, a game that's now found in many casinos. *Multistrike Poker* has four levels of hands, each of which is worth twice as much as the last. In order to advance from one level to another, though, you must either win the previous hand or get a "Free Ride"—a feature that's random. This is a tricky game, because your strategy on the bottom rows must be adjusted to allow you to reach your objective, which is to advance to the next level. (Specifically, your strategy must be more conservative on the lower levels because of the need to get *any* winning hand.) Moreover, because this game has four levels of hands, you'll potentially be betting 20 coins rather than 5. And as you might expect, failure to bet the maximum number of coins is a mistake, because this will prevent you from advancing to the next level. The fact is that many people have a hard time remaining within their budget when they play a Multistrike game. Again, this doesn't mean that you should avoid Multistrike Poker. If your budget permits, and if you find a full-pay video poker game that you know how to play, it may be a very good choice for you. But be realistic about the chunk of change that this game can bite out of your gambling budget.

Although I've discussed just two casino options that can be budget breakers, keep in mind that manufacturers are always coming up with new video poker games that are fun and exciting, but potentially expensive. And casinos are always more than happy to make these games available. It's up to you, the savvy player, to learn all you can about a game *before* you deposit your money in the machine.

COMMONSENSE TIPS

By now, you should have a clear idea of both proper budgeting and smart game selection. But there are a few more things you should keep in mind if you want to get the most play you can get out of your bankroll and, if you're lucky, return home with more money than you took with you.

Don't Play Intoxicated or Tired

Free drinks have long been a part of casino gambling. As long as you keep playing, drinks are complimentary. But realize that casinos provide drinks not just as a means of enticing you to stay longer, but also to cloud your judgment. Always remember that video poker relies on the ability to make rational decisions, and all those playing strategies you learned and practiced will go out the window after a few drinks. To play smart, you'll want to steer clear of alcohol during your gambling sessions. Remember: Those drinks aren't free if they make you lose your bankroll.

Fatigue is as harmful as intoxication, and perhaps more common. Players who visit a casino—often after traveling a long distance to get there—want to do too much, too soon. There are no clocks or windows in most casinos, so it's easy to forget about time and get caught up in the glitz, glamour, and excitement of the casino. As a result, many players keep gambling even when exhausted, trying to get as much play in as possible. Anyone can see that this is a recipe for bad decisions and fast losses.

Never play tired. You'll enjoy yourself more and play with greater accuracy if you return to the casino when you're well rested.

The guidelines I've provided about sticking to your budget should help you to limit play. Nevertheless, as already discussed, it's wise to wear a watch and set a time limit for your gambling activities. This should prevent overbetting as well as poor playing.

Take Advantage of Slot Cards and Promotions

Earlier in the chapter, I warned you that casinos often pressure customers to keep playing just to win comps on their slot club cards. Nevertheless, as soon as you enter a new casino, you should apply for a slot club card, as use of the card will result in both comps and cash in most casinos.

Slot clubs were created in the early 1980s by Atlantic City casinos to keep players from moving from one casino to another. By offering complimentary services such as free rooms, food, shows, and even cash as a reward for customer loyalty, casinos were able to keep players coming back. Slot clubs are now found in most casinos, and in addition to the comps listed above, they also send customers information about their special promotions. Many clubs even give discount coupons and

Each casino determines the number of points you must earn to receive a certain amount of cash back. The slot club brochure will explain how use of your card can earn you cash, as well as various comps.

Gambling and Taxes

If you have spent any time in casinos, you may already know that the magic number—the number that requires a casino to report winnings to the IRS—is $1,199. That means that if a single jackpot exceeds that amount by as much as a dollar, you must claim it as income on your tax return. In fact, if you receive a jackpot of this size, the machine will automatically "lock-up," and you will get a "call attendant" message. The casino will then request your social security number and ask if you want the taxes removed directly from the jackpot. This decision is entirely up to you. However, when the attendant returns with the cash or check, you will be required to sign the W-2G form and the IRS will receive a matching copy. Your copy should be kept with your tax records.

You will be able to deduct your gambling *losses* as long as you itemize deductions rather than taking a standard deduction, and only up to the amount of your gambling winnings reported that year. The IRS suggests that you keep your records as a written log, and further advises you to use a small paper notepad or diary for this purpose. You may instead keep records of your wins and losses in your computer or Palm Pilot, but the IRS prefers paper, possibly because they want the records to be entered in your log "contemporaneously"—in other words, as soon after the win or loss as possible. Since you are not allowed to take electronic devices into the casino, contemporaneous computer logs are impossible. Aware of these preferences, many casinos will provide you with a free diary for tax records upon request.

Your record or "diary" should contain the following information:

❑ The name and address or location of the gambling establishment.

❑ The date of your gambling session.

❑ The denomination played.

free gifts just for filling out the club application. Finally, only if you have a slot club card will you be able to obtain a win/loss statement for your tax records. (To learn more about gambling and taxes, see the inset found above.)

How do you get a slot club card? First, look for the slot club booth. When you find it, ask for an application. You will be given a form on which you must supply your name, address, birthday, and sometimes your social security number. You may also be asked to produce picture identification, such as your driver's license. The form usually has a place for you to identify your gambling preferences, hobbies, and interests. While you're at the booth, ask for the brochure on the slot club so that you can learn about the various benefits offered. Also ask for *two*

The best incentive casinos offer is called *bounceback cash*. Designed to keep you "bouncing back" to that casino, this money is not subtracted from your cash point total.

❑ The amounts that you won and lost.

❑ The number of the video poker machine, if possible. (This is optional.)

Note that the IRS remains murky on what constitutes a gambling "session" for tax purposes. If you're on a vacation for a few days, you can use each day as a session, and follow up your daily records of wins and losses with your combined trip results. Just be sure to keep your records consistent and clear.

In the event of an audit, the more supporting documentation you have, the better. I advise you to request a win/loss statement from the casino at the end of the year. The casino will be able to supply you with this information as long as you have consistently used your slot club card. If you failed to use the card, though, this data won't be available.

Be aware, too, that the IRS will consider only the calendar year for which you are paying taxes. Heavy losses incurred during previous years will not be considered. And remember that the burden of proof of records is on *you*, not on the IRS.

If you are a Canadian citizen, you'll be happy to learn that a treaty between the United States and Canada entitles you to a refund of Federal tax monies removed from any gambling jackpots you win while in the US. Make sure to file a US Non-Resident Tax Return, which will enable you to get either a full or a partial refund of the amount withheld.

Finally, be aware that the same $1,199 threshold used by the IRS is also used by some states to deduct taxes. Sometimes the amount withheld is refundable, and sometimes it's not. Louisiana, for instance, deducts 6%, but refunds most of this income to nonresidents who file returns. Mississippi deducts 3% and Massachusetts deducts 5%, and in both cases, the money is nonrefundable. Because the tax laws vary greatly from state to state, you'll want to keep careful records and check with your accountant to learn the regulations in your area.

cards so that if you lose your card, you won't have to wait in line for a new one or play without a card if the club is closed.

Once you get your card, use it every time you play video poker. If you're using a newer machine, you'll see that the slots for the cards are built into the face of the machine. On older machines, the slot may be anywhere—in front, on the side, or on top. Usually, there are small yellow lights around the slot insertion area, making it easy to find. Consistent use of the card will allow the casino to track your play and award points that can be redeemed for cash, comps, or both. You will, in effect, be paid to play. Just don't let the attraction of comps seduce you into forgetting your budget. A free dinner is not worth the loss of your bankroll.

Video poker is a wonderfully exciting game—a great opportunity for you to exercise your skill and knowledge and, with some luck, enjoy big payoffs along the way. But without a plan of money management and some discipline, this game can instead rob you of your bankroll, and even erode your savings. I hope that the techniques presented in this chapter will help you enjoy the thrill of video poker and go home feeling like a winner.

SELECTING A CASINO

How should you choose a casino? The answer will vary, depending on your priorities and preferences. Do you plan to focus on gambling only, with the goal of winning as much money as possible? In addition to playing, do you hope to enjoy a beautiful casino that offers a variety of activities? Do you want to stay at the casino's hotel, or do you intend to choose your hotel and casino separately? Are you traveling alone? With your spouse? With your entire family? These are just a few of the considerations you may have in mind.

Because the goal of this book is to help you win at video poker, this chapter will emphasize that aspect of selecting a casino. But because many people have other considerations as well, ranging from the cost of accommodations to the availability of family-friendly activities, we'll also look at other topics of interest so that you can find the gambling experience that's right for you.

UNDERSTANDING THE DIFFERENT TYPES OF CASINOS

Gone are the days when gamblers had to head for Sin City to make a wager. Now the majority of states offer casinos, with some states hav-

Only two states—Hawaii and Utah—are without any form of legalized gambling.

ing only a handful, and a few states—California, Florida, Montana, Nevada, and Washington, for instance—offering well over a hundred.

One of the reasons casinos are now found in so many places is that over time, both entrepreneurs and politicians have found that these businesses are highly profitable. Now there are land-based commercial casinos, which are nontribal casinos primarily owned by corporations; Native American Indian casinos, which are owned by various tribes; riverboat casinos, which are located on the banks of a river or lake, but are no longer required to acutally cruise; racinos, which are casinos located in racetracks; noncasino retailers—restaurants, convenience stores, truck stops, and bars that have some casino games; cruise ship casinos; and online casinos. As the following discussions show, these establishments don't differ merely in terms of ownership, location, and appearance, but also in terms of the benefits and drawbacks they offer the video poker player.

Land-Based Commercial Casinos

Currently, land-based commercial casinos can be found in six states: Colorado, Louisiana, Michigan, Nevada, New Jersey, and South Dakota. From the start, it's important to understand that for the video poker player, all of these establishments have a distinct advantage over most other gaming establishments: *They are operated in state-regulated jurisdictions that require video poker machines to deal random card sequences.* (Think back to the random number generator discussed in Chapter 2.) This is due to a Nevada regulation, adopted by every other state with a gaming authority, that if dice or cards are used in a casino game, the electronic version must be as random as the real game, within computational limits set by certain tests performed by gaming authority agents.

While land-based commercial casinos have the above regulation in common, in other ways, they are often markedly different from one another. You see, the regulatory agency for each state has jurisdiction over all the commercial casinos operating there, and each state has its own mandates. Because of this, the gaming tax rates and mandated maximum and minimum expected returns (ERs) also differ from state to state—and this can have a major impact on players. Clearly, the more the casino has to pay in gaming taxes, the less money is available for player advantage games and comps. How do the maximum and minimum ERs affect the video poker player? Well, machines with positive (player advantage) ERs cannot legally be placed in any commercial casino if the state mandates require an upper limit of 100% or less. (To learn about expected returns—also called payback percentages—turn to page 48 of Chapter 3.)

To give you a more concrete idea of the differing state mandates that affect the gambling experience, I've created Table 5.1, which shows both the percentage of gaming taxes paid and the mandated minimum and maximum expected returns in the six states that have land-based commercial casinos. As you can see, Nevada and South Dakota are the only two states that do not place lids on what a land-based commercial casino can pay for either video poker or slots. These two states, then, are the only ones that can legally offer player advantage games—games that offer an expected return greater than 100% when video poker players use perfect or near-perfect strategy over a sufficiently long period of play.

Table 5.1. Gaming Taxes and Expected Returns in States With Land-Based Commercial Casinos

State	Gaming Taxes Paid	Expected Return
Colorado	20% maximum graduated tax.*	80 to 100%.
Louisiana	21.5%.	80 to 99%.
Michigan	24%.	80 to 100%.
Nevada	6.75% maximum graduated tax.*	75% minimum; no maximum.
New Jersey	8%.	83 to 99.99%.
South Dakota	8%.	80% minimum; no maximum.

* In states with graduated taxes, the gaming tax varies each year depending on the volume of business done by the casino. The tax can only go as high as the maximum percentage, though.

Does this mean that I recommend gambling only in Nevada and South Dakota? Definitely not, because the expected return is not the only factor that should be considered. New Jersey, for instance, has no maximum denominations of bills or maximum jackpot rules. This means that many of the games I recommend in Chapter 1 can be found in a variety of denominations. New Jersey casinos also offer a variety of comps (room, food, and beverages), promotional gifts, cash back, and a

When choosing a casino, you'll want to consider a number of factors. Is that casino required by the state to use machines with random number generators? Does the state allow it to provide good returns? Does it offer perks that can turn casino advantage games into player advantage games? Finally, does it offer the specific games that you want to play?

range of other perks. These perks—along with progressive jackpots—can make a significant difference in returns when playing video poker over a long period of time. In some cases, they can even add enough value to the pay schedule of a video poker game to turn a negative return into a positive return. (You'll learn more about comps and promotions on page 110. For information on progressive jackpots, see page 63 in Chapter 3.)

As you can see, I believe that land-based commercial casinos are an excellent choice for the video poker player. First and foremost, these casinos must use random number generators in their video poker machines, which means that the player can benefit from the use of smart strategies. Second, gaming authority agents check the video poker machines in these state-regulated casinos, making sure that they're offering the expected returns advertised. But as you've learned, some commercial casinos are better than others when it comes to video poker. So remember that every commercial casino is not giving you a great deal. When selecting a casino, it's smart to look at everything offered, from the games to the slot clubs.

Getting There

As you learned on page 95, casinos are now found all over the country. Perhaps you have a number of casinos in your area. If not, a neighboring city or state may offer what you're looking for. Or maybe you'd prefer a casino on the other side of the country. One thing is for sure: Once you settle on a destination, you'll have to get there.

When planning most vacations, people know they're going to foot their own transportation bill. But when it comes to a stay at a casino, it's important to remember that many casinos go to great lengths to attract customers, and one of the many ways they entice players is to offer discounted travel packages.

If you've chosen to spend just a day at a casino in a nearby community, look into casino-sponsored day trips. Often, you'll be able to travel to your casino of choice by bus for only a small fee. For this fee, you are likely to receive not only transportation but also a dining coupon and even a voucher that can be turned in for a small denomination of playing chips. The bus will take you to the casino in the morning, and after you spend the next five or six hours trying your luck, it will pick you up and take you back home.

Perhaps you're interested in a longer trip to a more distant location. If so, you may already know about the *gambling junket*—a package set up for groups of gamblers who are considered

Native American Indian Casinos

Since the late 1980s, when a series of court cases led to the right of American Indians to set up gaming houses, Indian tribes have used their position as sovereign entities to establish a large and ever-growing number of casinos. At this time, Indian casinos operate in twenty-nine states: Alabama, Alaska, Arizona, California, Colorado, Connecticut, Florida, Idaho, Iowa, Kansas, Louisiana, Michigan, Minnesota, Mississippi, Missouri, Montana, Nebraska, Nevada, New Mexico, New York, North Carolina, North Dakota, Oklahoma, Oregon, South Dakota, Texas, Washington, Wisconsin, and Wyoming. Not all of the tribal casinos, though, offer video poker. Presently, those in Alabama, Alaska, Missouri, Nebraska, Oklahoma, and Wyoming do *not* have video poker machines. If you come across games that look like video poker machines in those states' tribal casinos, you'll know that you've found a video lottery terminal (VLT). (See page 35 to learn about VLTs.)

Tribal casinos differ from commercial casinos in that, although the state where the casino is located must have an agreement with the tribe,

special guests of the hotel. Junkets first appeared in the 1960s, when Las Vegas casinos wanted to bring high rollers into their establishments from distant locations such as the East Coast. The junkets lasted for about four days and provided chartered jet service, limousines, hotel room charges, food, and beverages—all of which were free as long as long as the junket players kept gambling.

In the 1970s, casinos began offering junkets for low rollers. Now, junket programs for lower-stake gamblers usually include transportation, rooms, meals, etc., all of which are either "comped" (complimentary) or provided at a special casino rate based on amount of play. The comps offered are not as extravagant as those provided for high rollers, but are worth considering. Just be aware that players who do not gamble the required amount of time or do not make adequately high bets will forfeit some of the junket benefits. Be aware, too, that many junkets are scams set up by private companies for their own profit. You'll want to trust only those offered by the casinos directly to you.

If you are not interested in a day trip and do not qualify for a gambling junket, keep in mind that once you begin playing at a casino, you can start earning comps, which may eventually include free transportation for future trips. Believe it or not, some successful video poker players *never* pay their own plane fare when heading to their favorite casino.

these establishments are not regulated by the states. Instead, the responsibility for ensuring the integrity of gambling in these casinos rests with individual tribal governments. Moreover, as sovereign entities, the tribes are not required to make public information about how they regulate their casinos. Thus, players cannot always determine whether the video poker machines offered in Indian casinos deal random card sequences.

Because expected returns are dictated by the tribe's compact with the state in which it is located, these percentages vary from state to state. In fact, some states have a separate agreement with each tribe within their borders, so percentages can even vary within a single state. Table 5.2 shows the expected returns of those states whose tribal casinos offer video poker *and* were willing to make these returns known to the public. Note that unlike Table 5.1, this one has no column listing the gaming taxes paid to the state. That's because states cannot impose taxes or fees on Indian gambling, except for fees to which the tribe agrees. In fact, this has been an area of continuing controversy, with some states demanding—but not necessarily receiving—a share of the action.

Table 5.2. Expected Returns in States With Tribal Casinos

State	Expected Return	State	Expected Return
Arizona	83 to 100%.	New Mexico	80% minimum.
Florida	No minimum.	North Carolina	83 to 98%.
Iowa	80 to 99%.	North Dakota	83 to 100%.
Michigan	75% minimum.	Oregon	No minimum.
Minnesota	83 to 98%.	Washington	75%.
Montana	No minimum.	Wisconsin	80 to 100%.

As you can see by looking at Table 5.2, many states—Minnesota and North Carolina, for instance—have a dismal range of expected returns, which precludes them from offering any of the games I recommend in earlier chapters. And the tribal casinos in some states, such as Florida, have *no* minimums at all, truly leaving the public at the mercy of the management.

In all respects, Indian casinos run the gamut from dreadful to excellent. You've already seen that they offer a wide range of expected returns—although in general, their returns are not as good as those offered in some state-regulated establishments. And while some have no amenities, others are as lavish as the pleasure palaces on the Vegas Strip, with beautiful hotels, luxurious spas, upscale shops, shows, restaurants, and more. If you are interested in a tribal casino, my advice is that you check it out as much as possible before you spend your hard-earned money there. Speak to players who have spent time there. Visit the casino and examine the games and pay tables, comparing them to the pay charts included in this book so that you can quickly spot player advantage games. And always keep in mind that their video poker machines may or may not include the random number generators you can count on in most commercial casinos. (The inset on video lottery terminals, found on page 35 of Chapter 2, will help you identify states whose tribal casinos may *not* use random number generators.)

Riverboat Casinos

In 1989, Iowa and Illinois legalized riverboat casinos, and in 1991, Iowa launched the first gaming vessel in recent United States history. Now, riverboat casinos are legal in six states—Illinois, Indiana, Iowa, Louisiana, Mississippi, and Missouri. The type of gaming allowed on these floating casinos varies by jurisdiction. Note that the only state with both land-based commercial casinos and riverboat casinos is Louisiana. The other five states have only riverboat casinos.

Modern riverboat casinos were originally a means of selling casino gambling to voters who were not wild about the idea of gambling being legalized in their state. By physically limiting gambling to the river-boats, and also to the two- or three-hour period during which the boat would cruise down a river or around a lake or bay, promoters made gambling seem under control and isolated. Players could not spend all day and night in these casinos, nor could they lose as much as they might if the time were unrestricted. In fact, when the first riverboat casinos began operating in Iowa on April Fools Day in 1991, passengers were limited to $5 per bet with a maximum loss of $200 per person, per cruise.

When riverboats operating in the state of Illinois didn't impose Iowa's restrictions on wagers and losses, people flocked to Illinois' floating casinos, greatly cutting into the profitability of the Iowa boats.

As a result, early in 1994, the Iowa legislature voted to eliminate its gambling restrictions. Little by little, as gambling was better received by the various states involved, the riverboat casino changed. Nowadays, there is no requirement that these casinos cruise, and while some are actually boats, others are on a floating, but not navigable, platform.

Riverboat casinos are considered a commercial form of casino, and as such, their video poker machines must have random number generators that deal random card sequences. Like land-based commercial casinos, each riverboat casino must also follow its state's mandates regarding gaming taxes paid and minimum and maximum expected returns. Riverboat casinos also offer progressive jackpots and other promotions—perks that can improve the returns of a game. So on the surface, riverboat casinos *seem* like a great place to play video poker.

Unfortunately, though, riverboat casinos tend to be taxed at a higher rate than land-based casinos; often must pay local taxes as well as state taxes; and are charged an additional *admission tax*—a tax for each person who enters the casino. (See Table 5.3 for details.) While the admission tax may or may not be passed on directly to the customer in the form of an admission charge, the result of all of these fees is that riverboat casinos cannot offer the games recommended in earlier chapters, making these casinos a poor choice for the player who's looking for a positive game. Note that this is true even in the case of states that show a maximum expected return of 100%. Because they must pay such stiff taxes, these floating casinos simply can't offer ERs that come close to their max.

Table 5.3. **Gaming Taxes and Expected Returns in States With Riverboat Casinos**

State	Gaming Taxes and Other Fees	Expected Return
Illinois	15 to 70% graduated tax,* plus admission tax.	80 to 100%.
Indiana	15 to 35% graduated tax,* plus admission tax.	Not available.
Iowa	22% maximum graduated tax,* plus admission tax.	80 to 100%.
Louisiana	21.5%, plus admission tax and local tax.	80 to 99%.
Mississippi	8% maximum graduated tax,* plus admission tax and local tax.	80 to 100%.
Missouri	20%, plus admission tax.	80% minimum; no maximum.

*In states with graduated taxes, the gaming tax varies each year depending on the volume of business done by the casino. In states with a maximum percentage, though, the tax can't increase beyond the stated percentage.

Racinos

A combination of a racetrack and a casino, the *racino* has grown in popularity and numbers since Iowa authorized its first racino in 1994. Racetracks love them because they bring more people and revenue to the tracks, which have suffered losses due to declining interest in horse and dog racing. Politicians love them because they generate tax revenue for local and state governments, and because they don't involve the construction of new facilities. Right now, racinos are located in eight states: Delaware, Iowa, Louisiana, Maine, New Mexico, New York, Rhode Island, and West Virginia. Many more states are considering some form of racino legislation.

Racinos do not have table games, but limit themselves to electronic gambling devices, including slots and video poker machines. Unfortunately, though, the racino is *not* a good place to play video poker. As you may remember from Chapter 2, in most or all cases, the machines found in these facilities are video lottery terminals, or VLTs—not video poker machines with random number generators. For that reason, no amount of skill and strategy can help you win these games, as the winners are determined by a computerized lottery system. (For more information on VLTs, see the inset on page 35.) So while racinos may be a boon to racetrack owners and flagging state economies, they are no bargain for the video poker player.

Don't be seduced by terms like "state-regulated" and "random." A video poker machine can be state-regulated, but still provide low returns. A video lottery machine may be termed "random" because it chooses winners at random, but that doesn't mean that it uses a random number generator or that the use of smart playing strategies will have any effect on the outcome of the game. To get the winning edge, you have to find a machine with a random number generator *and* a positive expected return.

Noncasino Retailers—Bars, Restaurants, Convenience Stores, and Truck Stops

At this time, six states—Louisiana, Montana, New Mexico, Oregon, South Dakota, and West Virginia—have legalized video poker and other forms of electronic gambling in bars, convenience stores, truck stops, and fast-food restaurants. Several additional states now have proposals to legalize gaming devices in these venues. And in many more states—Indiana, Kentucky, and Georgia among them—although it is *not* legal to have gaming machines in these establishments, hundreds of video poker machines are nonetheless found in bars and the like, as well as in fraternal organizations.

Much has been written about the problems posed by both legal and illegal gaming machines found in retail noncasinos. State authorities, for instance, complain that it is impossible to locate and shut down all the illegal gambling machines that are out there. My advice on these machines is simple: Stay away! As first discussed in Chapter 2, nearly all of the video poker machines found in these establishments are VLTs, which should always be avoided. This is true of both the legal and illegal machines. While the machines in some states are state regulated, that doesn't mean that they have random number generators or that their payout rates are anything but dismal. And when illegal machines are involved, payout rates hit rock bottom—about 55 to 60 percent, meaning that they will cough up only 55 to 60 cents for every dollar wagered over the life of the machine.

On a two-day trip down the length of Interstate 75 in Kentucky, one reporter found well over a hundred illegal gambling machines located in truck stops, convenience stores, and fast-food restaurants.

Cruise Ship Casinos

At one time, cruises were one of the few places where American players could find casino gambling outside of Las Vegas and Atlantic City. A cruise ship would leave port, and the casino would open as soon as the ship was three miles offshore in international waters. (Interestingly, the three-mile limit was originally set as the boundary of the United States because it was the maximum distance that shore-based cannons could fire.)

In the last few decades, casinos have become increasingly available on shore, as several states have approved riverboat gambling, additional states have licensed traditional land-based casinos, and American Indian tribes have used their sovereign nation status to open casinos. No longer do players have to turn to cruise ships to satisfy the gambling itch. But by no means are cruise ship casinos in danger of losing their popularity. Many vacationers now consider casinos an essential feature of the cruise experience, and cruise lines—responding to customer enthusiasm and high profits—are building bigger and more elaborate onboard casinos than ever before. Almost all of the well known, heavily marketed vacation cruise companies now operate casinos aboard their liners.

Cruise ship casinos have proven to be absolute gold mines for the cruise lines. They cater to vacationers who have expendable income, are geared up for fun and excitement, and, in most cases, are not knowledgeable enough to separate good gambling conditions from bad.

How does gambling on a cruise ship compare with gambling in a commercial casino? On the upside, a cruise ship casino can be a less intimidating introduction to gambling. Because cruise lines recognize that most passengers are not big-time players, but regard gambling as a small piece of the cruise experience, dealers and other casino workers are more patient than their commercial-casino counterparts, and more willing to help beginners learn the games.

On the downside, cruise ship casinos are very different from riverboat and land-based commercial casinos, which are subject to strict regulations and disclosure requirements. Casinos that float in international waters are pretty much given license to do as they please. While they are supposed to follow the guidelines prepared in 1999 by an industry trade association called the International Council of Cruise Lines (ICCL), these guidelines demand neither minimum expected returns nor video poker machines that have random number generators. Many experts feel that the guidelines are designed to protect the cruise line, not the consumer. Most important, cruise ships are notorious for offering poor pay tables with low expected returns.

What's the bottom line on cruise ship casinos? If you love the cruise ship experience, you may consider a minor investment in some gaming fun while you're at sea. But if you're a serious player, you will probably want to avoid gambling aboard these floating hotels, and by no means should you or anyone else risk losing a large sum of money during your cruising vacation.

Online Casinos

Perform an Internet search for "online casinos" and you'll find unlimited opportunities to play any casino game, including video poker, in the privacy of your own home on your own computer. In fact, online casinos are so eager to get your business that even a search for "casinos"—forget the word "online"—will quickly lead you to several Internet gambling sites.

No one needs to have the attractions of an online casino explained to him. Like every other online service, it's convenient. There's no need to go to Vegas or Atlantic City to gamble, and no need to take a day (or week) off from work to try your luck. You can play video poker whenever you have a few minutes—even in the middle of the night. You can also explore a host of online casinos before deciding where you feel comfortable enough to place your bets. You can even gamble with "free money" so that you can learn the rules of the game and decide whether or not you want to bet for real. Want to use strategy cards or training software? Nobody's there to stop you.

Because most people patronize cruise ships only occasionally—and perhaps only once in a lifetime—the lines have no reason to create a climate that promotes customer loyalty and return business. A few cruise ship casinos now offer cash back for slot club points, but you can't redeem these points until your next trip!

Unfortunately, there are also a number of problems with online gambling. First, the online casino gambler runs the risk of feeling too secure in his own home, and may not recognize that the stakes he is gambling with are in no way lower than if he were in a conventional casino. While the environment of a brick-and-mortar casino is a continual reminder that this is a business—specifically, a business that's trying to get your money—a game played on a home computer while sitting in your living room, bedroom, or study may seem like a comparatively innocent and benign pursuit.

Another problem—a big one, from my point of view—is that online casinos are unregulated by the United States government. In fact, they are all operated from *outside* the United States. Although this may change in the future, at this time, playing video poker in an online casino is a risky business—in more ways than one. Some Internet players tell stories of never being paid after winning bets, or of being paid only after lodging a complaint and enduring long delays. In fact, payment options in general are scarce. Because of pressure from the Justice Department, the escrow agent PayPal stopped processing payments for online gambling in 2002, and many banks are now declining credit card transactions from these casinos.

And then there's the question of legality. At this point, United States laws regarding online gambling are unclear. Several states—Nevada, Louisiana, Michigan, and Illinois—have outlawed online gambling. And, of course, some states ban gambling of any type. But at the same time, no *federal* law prohibits American citizens from gambling online. Moreover, neither state governments nor the federal government has the means to prevent, halt, or prosecute this form of gambling.

If you feel drawn to online gambling sites, I can only tell you to be careful. If possible, speak to other people who have used a particular site before using it yourself. Then proceed slowly so that you won't get badly burned by any less-than-scrupulous sites. Finally, if you are concerned about the legality of online gambling, check the laws in your state or region before entering an online casino.

FINDING THE BEST MACHINES AND GAMES

In Chapters 1 and 3, I recommend specific video poker games and provide information on choosing the best versions of those games. It's important that you grasp the concepts explained in those chapters—concepts like expected return and volatility—before assessing the games offered by various casinos and choosing the casino in which you want to play. By all means, consider the "fun factor" since you're there to have a good time, not to earn a living. But if you are going to make your bankroll last as long as possible—and hopefully hit a jackpot or two—you'll want to pick a game for which you have proven strategies, and use your pay charts to ensure that it's the best-paying version of that game.

Years ago, Las Vegas was the home of high-paying video poker machines, while Atlantic City had poorer-paying machines. Gradually, competition—and smart players who recognized a bad pay table when they saw one—forced Atlantic City to offer better games. At the same time, an increasing number of skilled players cut into casino profits, placing pressure on Las Vegas casinos to lower their pay tables. In general, full-pay video poker machines are getting harder and harder to find everywhere.

Unless you know someone who has recently played video poker in your location of interest, you'll probably have to visit different casinos and see what they have to offer before you find what you want. Don't expect to get the information you need by phoning the casinos or checking their websites; the casinos are not about to provide you with specific information on their games. The few casinos that advertise player advantage games are often cagey about divulging their exact location, so you will have to conduct a thorough search. Even if you played in a casino once before, using good-paying machines, keep in mind that gaming establishments are constantly moving machines from one place to another—sometimes to areas that they believe you will be unlikely to explore. Players have told me stories of searching for full-pay machines only to find them in noisy areas under construction or smoke-filled sections of the casinos. So, again, you'll have to look for the good machines.

It's not always easy to find good-paying versions of the video poker games you want to play. In most cases, you'll have to visit different casinos and see what they have to offer, carefully comparing the casino pay tables with your own pay charts.

Of course, experienced video poker players can walk into a casino and quickly determine if it offers good opportunities. But if you're just starting to learn about video poker, a new casino may be a bit intimidating, and you may find it difficult to discover if it has what you're looking for. Here are some simple ways to identify a casino that provides player advantage choices.

❑ **Look for the games recommended in Chapters 1 and 3.** I have recommended these games not only because they're widely available, but also because they offer good expected returns and are easy to play with the strategies provided in this book. Just be sure to compare the pay tables on the machines to the pay charts provided on pages 54 to 56 to ensure that you have found the best-paying versions available.

❑ **Seek out quarter machines.** These days, most full-pay games are found in quarter denominations, so if you find a game you know how to play on a quarter machine, you can be pretty certain you've found a good game.

❑ **Search for 9/6 Jacks or Better.** Yes, this is just *one* of the games I recommend in this book, but as I said in Chapter 1, it's a great game for beginners. It's easy to play correctly, and it will allow you to play for a longer period of time on a limited budget. This is often the best game found in large denominations—dollars and higher—if you're interested in making larger bets. True, the ER is only 99.54%, but with cash bonuses or progressives, the full-pay version quickly becomes a positive game.

❑ **Keep an eye out for progressives.** As explained in Chapter 3, progressive games link several video poker machines together and use a portion of each bet made at these machines to feed a jackpot, which grows until a player gets the designated hand and wins the pot. These jackpots can make a big difference in a machine's payback percentage. If you want to know the math, see pages 64 to 67 in Chapter 3. If you're not interested in the details, just remember this: When you see a large progressive jackpot, go for it—and be sure to play max coins so that you'll get the best payout if you draw a Royal Flush.

❑ **Evaluate slot club offers.** In Chapter 4, I advised you to find the slot club booth as soon as you enter a new casino. There, you will be able to fill in an application and obtain a brochure, which will detail the benefits offered to members. You'll know that the casino provides good opportunities for you, the video poker player, if it offers:

• The same amount of points for video poker as for slots.

• Points on full-pay video poker machines.

- Both cash back and comp points.

- Cash back that is paid on the same day it's earned.

- Double or triple points on certain days.

- Discounts when using comp points.

- "Bounceback" cash—cash that is not part of the point balance.

❏ **Look for special promotions.** Sometimes, a casino will run a special promotion for a day or two. It may, for instance, offer bonus money if you get a specific Four of a Kind combination. If a great promotion is underway during your casino visit, you'll know that you've prob-

---

How Do Cash Back Offers Affect a Game's Expected Return?

In several chapters of this book, I point out that cash back offers can actually increase the ER of a game, and should therefore be considered when deciding if a game is worth playing. Fortunately, it's relatively easy to compute how cash back can boost an ER. Here are the steps you'll want to follow:

1. Multiply the cost of each point by the amount of points required to earn the cash back. This is your coin-in—the total amount of money you will wager.

2. Divide the cash back amount by the coin-in required to earn it.

3. Convert the result of Step 2 to a percentage by moving the decimal point two places to the right.

4. Add the result of Step 3 to the game's ER, and you'll have the game's new ER.

Let's say that you've found a game of Not-So-Ugly Deuces Wild that has an ER of 99.73%. The casino is offering $5 cash back for every 100 points earned, and it takes $25 to earn each point. Let's use our formula to determine the new ER.

1. Multiply the cost of each point—in this case, $25—by the amount of points required to earn the cash back—100 points. The result is $2,500. ($25 × 100 = $2,500) This is your coin-in.

2. Divide the cash back—$5—by $2,500. The result is .002. ($5 ÷ $2,500 = .002)

3. Convert .002 to a percentage by moving the decimal point two places to the right. The result is .2%.

4. Add .2% to the game's ER of 99.73%. The result—99.93%—is the game's new ER. (99.73% + .2% = 99.93%)

While in the above example, the increase in ER may not seem significant, it would definitely make a difference over the long term. Keep in mind, too, that if the points for this game were doubled, the ER would be 100.13%, making this a positive game. Moreover, the cash back would be *additional* to any comps earned during play.

ably found the right place to play video poker—for the length of the promotion, at least. (For more on promotions, see below.)

❑ **Be alert to good finds.** Sometimes, you may come across a payout that's even *better* than those recommended in Chapter 1. For example, 10/6 Double Double Bonus Poker, although rare, has been spotted in Nevada casinos. Always be on the lookout for a great game like this, and use your strategy cards to make the most of unexpected opportunities.

Finally, remember that it's up to you, the savvy player, to find the great games and offers. Locating the best machines is an important step in getting the video poker edge.

LOOKING FOR COMPS AND PROMOTIONS

Be sure to apply for a slot club card and to use it every time you play video poker. The points you earn can be redeemed for cash, comps, or both.

As discussed above, one of the easiest and smartest ways to get an edge on the casinos in terms of cold, hard cash is to play the comp game and take advantage of all the *perks*—short for *perquisites*—that each gaming establishment offers. The fact is that comps (room, food, and beverages), promotional gifts, cash back, and a range of other perks can make a significant difference in returns when playing video poker over a long period of time. That's why it's so important to choose a casino that makes outstanding offers.

In Chapter 3, I explained how a progressive jackpot can increase the expected return (ER) of a game. Well, a cash back offer can do the same thing. If you want to learn how a particular cash back offer will increase a game's ER, look at the inset on page 109, where I explain the easy-to-use formula you'll need to know.

Even before you set foot in a casino, you can learn a little about its offers by visiting its website. There you'll find basic information about its players club, and you'll be able to read about upcoming promotions. For instance, a quick visit to a local casino's website may show you that it will soon have a double-point day—a day on which anyone with a players club card will receive twice the usual number of points when playing a game at the casino. Be aware, though, that once you become a member of a players club, you will receive notices of these promotions by mail, and will no longer have to check the casino's website for these offers.

When you actually enter a casino, you can get more detailed information about its players club rules and policies by stopping by the desk that offers club applications. Usually, the staff will be willing to give you a copy of the policy and explain how the points you receive while

Video Poker Tournaments

To attract new customers and reward existing ones, casinos periodically offer tournaments—not only for video poker, but for many different casino games. While some require a fee to participate, others are free of charge to the casino's best customers. When no fee is charged, players stand to lose only their time, of course. When a fee is involved, players must compare the cost of the tournament with the benefits that may be gained by participating.

Video poker tournaments are usually held for one to two days, with each participant playing in one or more short sessions of about fifteen minutes' duration. Each player is given an equal number of credits at the start of each session. (Tournament play does not use cash or coins.) Participants then play at video poker machines whose pay tables have been adjusted for the event, usually with the use of a specially designed "tournament chip." The screen displays a Session Timer, which keeps track of the amount of time left in the session; a Credit Countdown, which keeps track of the player's remaining credits; and a Win Counter, which shows the points accumulated throughout the session, adding points for each winning hand, but not subtracting them for losing hands. The player who accumulates the most points during all of his sessions wins the video poker tournament. Note that players do *not* get to cash in their credits.

Tournaments are usually set up to pay a quarter to a half of the participants, so when there is an entry fee, a good number of players at least get their money back, and maybe earn a small profit. Competitors usually also receive comped meals, as well as small gifts such as t-shirts and mugs. And, of course, the winner is awarded a cash prize ranging from $1,000 to several thousand dollars. Occasionally, the winner gets as much as $25,000.

If you have spent time honing your video poker skills, you may be eager for the challenge of a tournament. Just be aware that if your goal is to win, and not just to compete, you will have to play both quickly and accurately. To prepare for the tournament, be sure to call the tournament organizer and get a copy of the rules and pay table well in advance so that you can adjust your computer tutorial program and practice at home. (See page 80 for information on tutorials.) Don't skip this step, as home practice is essential! The fast pace of a tournament makes it impossible to use strategy cards, so you'll have to *know* your strategies. Then try to arrive early, not only to avoid missing your assigned session but also to watch a round being played, as this will familiarize you with the process and enable you to compete with greater confidence. And remember: Speed is rewarded, so try to get in as many hands as possible during each tournament session.

playing will translate into free or discounted rooms, meal vouchers, show tickets, or cash back.

If you plan on spending a good deal of time on the casino floor, be sure to introduce yourself to the casino host, who has the ability to evaluate comp status and approve comps. A good way to meet the host is to first play a few games to get some credit, and then press the *Change/Call Attendant* button. When the attendant arrives at the machine, tell him that you want to speak to the casino host. Then ask the host about the casino's policy regarding room and food comps, and see if you qualify for any at that time. Be aware that casino hosts can sometimes use "discretionary comps," meaning that you can receive a service free of charge without reducing your comp account. At the end of your conversation, be sure to ask for the host's business card so that you can contact him on later trips.

It makes sense to learn what you can about each casino's offers. By checking websites and visiting several casinos, you'll be able to compare different policies, learn about promotions, and choose the casino with the best perks.

ASSESSING THE CASINO ENVIRONMENT

Anyone who's ever seen a movie depiction of a casino knows that it's a busy, noisy place with flashing lights, shouting players, clattering coins, ringing bells, and whining sirens. But beyond the lights and noise, every casino has its own individual character. So unless your sole concern is finding the best-paying video poker machines or the most generous comp program, you'll want to consider the casino environment before picking a place to play.

An important consideration for nearly everyone is safety. Unless you're staying in a resort casino and never intend to leave the casino complex, you'll want to choose a casino in a safe area. It's likely that you'll at least occasionally leave the casino late at night—hopefully with some cash!—and you'll want to feel that you are in no danger. Be sure to check this out in the daylight, rather than getting an unpleasant surprise after dark. (See Chapter 6 for more about safety.)

Is a smoke-free environment important to you? By and large, casinos are smoky places. Now, though, some casinos are catering to nonsmokers by offering nonsmoking floors, nonsmoking rooms, or sepa-

If you're staying and playing in the same casino, request a casino entrance room, if available. This means that you won't have to leave the building to get to your room. If you're staying elsewhere, and you have been lucky enough to win a large sum of money, ask security to walk you to your car when you leave for the night. Remember that the staff is there not just to protect the casino, but also to protect *you*.

rate nonsmoking casinos. If this is of interest to you, call ahead or perform a computer search to see if the casinos in your chosen location have no-smoke sections. If they do, before you decide to settle in for a long playing session, you'll want to visit the casinos and take a whiff. Sometimes a section is free of smokers, but not free of drifting smoke from nearby rooms.

Every casino crowd has its own character, and chances are, you'll be more comfortable in some groups than others. A search of casino websites will clue you into the type of clientele you're likely to find at each establishment. For instance, the upscale Bellagio, with it's hand-blown glass lobby ceiling and art gallery, is likely to attract a clientele that's quite different from that of Circus Circus, which boasts not only an ongoing circus but also an RV park. With which group of players would you feel most at ease? Only you can decide.

Finally, some casinos are so packed with players that although they may offer great games, you will never get near them. And, of course, some times of the year are busier than others. If you hate crowds—as well as the higher room rates that often accompany high demand—you'll want to read the inset on page 114 and schedule your casino visits accordingly.

Even the best casino can be a nightmare during holidays, on weekends, and at certain other times of the year. The inset on page 114 will help you schedule your vacation for a time when hotel rates are good, and high-paying video poker machines are more accessible.

CHOOSING ACCOMMODATIONS

If you've already visited some casino websites as suggested earlier in this chapter, you've learned that while some casinos are attached to full resorts, others are stand-alone gaming establishments with no accommodations. If you're visiting a casino for more than a day, this is another area that should be considered.

Many people love the ease of staying and playing in the same place, and may never leave their chosen casino's complex of restaurants, shops, and theaters during their trip. But keep in mind that you don't have to stay at the Bellagio to see the beautiful fountain show, nor do you have to book a room at the Borgata to either shop or dine there. So if a particular casino has the games and other attractions you want, but offers either no accommodations or accommodations that are not to your liking, don't hesitate to book your room in one place and play in another. Just make sure that your hotel is reasonably close to your casino or that you have a convenient means of transportation.

The Best and Worst Times to Visit a Casino

While many people love the exhilaration of a crowded casino, many more feel frustrated when hordes of players prevent them from using the best-paying video poker machines, from focusing on playing strategies, and from getting a good room rate. When are casinos most crowded? Although it can vary from city to city, you'll probably want to avoid the following times:

❑ **Major holidays.** The most crowded days of the year are usually New Year's Eve, Memorial Day, the Fourth of July, and Labor Day. Most people have these days off and are in a celebratory mood, making the casinos both congested and noisy. Because many people spend Christmas and Thanksgiving with family, casinos are less crowded during these holidays.

❑ **Monday nights during the football season.** As you might expect, Monday night football draws a rowdy crowd. Super Bowl Sunday is another time when casinos are packed.

❑ **Major conventions.** When a convention is in town, hotels and casinos are crowded, room rates are higher, and traffic is miserable. So before visiting a casino, use an Internet search to check that city's convention schedule, or call your hotel of choice and ask if anything is going on during the dates of your planned visit. You'll be glad you did.

❑ **Local events.** Like conventions, special events—the National Rodeo Finals in Las Vegas, for instance—mean mobs of people and inflated prices. Again, a quick Internet search or a phone call to a local hotel can help you avoid particularly hectic dates.

❑ **Weekends.** As you might expect, since most people are free over the weekend, that's when casinos are most congested and most likely to jack up their prices.

When are the *best* times to visit a casino? Consider the following options:

❑ **Weekdays.** If you can manage a weekday trip, you'll usually have greater access to full-pay games and get far better room rates. You'll also find it easier to get a comped room.

❑ **Your birthday.** Did you know that many casinos offer all kinds of special perks on your birthday, ranging from free meals and bonus slot points to cash and gifts? This is why it's so important to provide your date of birth when joining the slot club and to always keep your ID on hand. When the time comes, you'll be expected to *prove* that it's your birthday.

❑ **Your wedding anniversary.** Like your birthday, your wedding anniversary will mean offers of comped meals, gifts, and cash from certain casinos. Again, you'll want to include this information on every slot club application you fill out.

❑ **The off-season.** In most regions, some seasons are more popular than others, and by visiting during the off-season—during the intense heat of a Las Vegas summer, for instance—you can avoid crowds and save money. Area hotels should be able to pinpoint the off-season for you.

It takes a little planning and research to choose the best time for a casino visit. But when you enjoy your vacation and come home a winner, you'll realize that your efforts were more than worthwhile.

Remember, too, that if a casino's hotel is a bit beyond your budget, by playing in the casino and diligently using your players club card, you can build up points that may, in the future, allow you to stay there at a reduced rate, or even free of charge. So if a certain hotel is attractive to you, consider the option of patronizing its casino for future perks— as long as it offers the games you're looking for. It doesn't make much sense to lose $1,000 playing unfamiliar games on low-paying machines in order to comp a $500 room.

Finally, if you're traveling with your family, you'll want to look for casinos that offer family-friendly activities and services. The Mohegan Sun has extensive child-care facilities, while Harrahs does not have a child-care facility, but will make child-care arrangements when requested. And of course some casinos, like Circus Circus, are known for kid-oriented attractions ranging from live circus acts to carnival games and a theme park.

IN CONCLUSION

These days, the range of casinos is truly amazing. They're found in all areas of the country—in busy cities, on isolated Indian reservations, and even on lakes and rivers. And they come in all forms. While some casinos are lavish full-service resorts offering an array of adult entertainments, others are geared more for families, and still others are relatively small stand-alone gaming establishments that provide no additional attractions beyond perhaps a restaurant.

When choosing a casino, it's easy to be seduced by the many options and by all the hype and dazzle. But if you want to go home a winner, it's important to keep your eye on the ball—or in this case, on the pay table, the comps, and the jackpots. That's what gives a savvy player the video poker edge.

CASINO ETIQUETTE AND SAFETY

I f you've finished reading Chapters 1 through 5, you already know a good deal about how to choose a casino, how to select a good video poker machine, and how to play the video poker game you've chosen. But if you plan to visit a commercial, riverboat, tribal, or cruise ship casino, you have to know more. You have to know the do's and don'ts of playing etiquette, and you have to understand how you can safeguard both yourself and your possessions—including any winnings—not only in the casino, but also when leaving after a gambling session.

Is there anything complicated about casino protocol and safety? Absolutely not. In most cases, it just involves using a little common sense. But the fact remains that every day, people get into unnecessary arguments—either with other players or with casino personnel—or lose money and other valuables to thieves and pickpockets. And it doesn't have to happen. By following the guidelines presented in this chapter, you will be among the many players who, by taking a few precautions, are able to enjoy a safe and pleasant casino experience.

CASINO ETIQUETTE

You probably never think about it, but every place you go, from the office to the supermarket, requires a certain behavior—a certain etiquette. When paying for groceries, you wouldn't think of dividing your order between two checkout counters just so you could get out of the store faster. Similarly, you should never play two machines at once or to do a host of other things that can cause problems on the casino floor.

As you may have guessed, the etiquette I'm about to discuss has less to do with social convention and more to do with being fair to other players, making things run smoothly for everyone involved, and following basic casino rules. The guidelines aren't many, but they are important. Let's take a look at them.

Make Sure That a Machine Is Free Before You Start Playing

Because players sometimes step away from the machines they're using—to visit the rest room or for a number of other reasons—a machine that is unattended is not necessarily free. And as you might guess, if you start playing a machine that someone else is still using, you will be in for a fight when the other person returns.

So when you come upon a machine that appears to be free, always check to see if there are any coins in the tray, credits on the meter, or a players club card inserted in the slot. If there are, look for another machine. What if there are no free machines and the previous player hasn't returned after a long wait? In that case, contact a member of the casino staff and explain the situation so that she can determine if it's okay for you to play. If there are credits on the machine, the casino can even cash out and keep the ticket safe until the player returns.

Don't "Save" Your Machine for More Than a Few Minutes

If you return to a video poker machine and find that someone else has begun playing—with your credits still on the meter—contact the casino staff as quickly as possible. A mechanic may be able to determine when the other player's cash was inserted in the machine.

After reading the scenario above, it should be clear that if you have to leave your machine, but you intend to return and continue playing, you should stay away for the shortest time possible—no more than fifteen minutes. It's inconsiderate to "reserve" a machine for a longer period of time when there are other people who'd like to play, and a scarcity of good machines. Also realize that if your machine is unattended, despite any precautions you might take, there's always the chance that someone will seize the opportunity to start playing, possibly with your credits.

What's the best way to "save" a machine if you have to step away for a few minutes? For many years, players would place a plastic coin cup over the handle of the machine or on their seat to indicate that they intended to return. Because the newer ticket-in ticket-out (TITO) machines don't have coin cups, you usually won't have that option. Instead, you can lean your chair against the machine, if it's the type of chair that can be moved; ask another player or a casino employee to watch your machine for you; or leave an ash tray or article of clothing on the chair. But keep in mind that none of these strategies will stop the person who's truly determined to play your machine. Also remember that casino staff is busy, and that other players are more interested in their own pursuits than in yours, so it's unrealistic to expect someone else to diligently guard your machine for you. If you're going to step away for just a few minutes, you can chance it. If you plan to take a longer break, both common sense and consideration for others dictate that you cash out and remove your club card from the machine.

Be aware that as far as the casino is concerned, once you leave the machine you're playing—for any reason at all—the machine is considered abandoned.

Play Only One Machine at a Time

In most casinos, signs over the video poker machines specify "One machine per player during peak hours," or something to that effect. Nevertheless, there's always a player who uses two or more machines at once while other casino goers are unable to find a free machine. While you can't control the actions of other people, you can control your own, so I strongly suggest that you play only one video poker machine at a time. This will not only give other people a chance to play, but will also enable you to focus on your strategies, which is what this book is all about. After all, it doesn't make much sense to play two machines if you're going to lose money on both of them due to lack of focus.

What can you do if another player is using several machines? First, politely ask her to let you use one. If she refuses, notify casino management and ask them to take the next step.

Be Aware That Chairs Are at a Premium

When playing at a video poker machine, it may be tempting to use the vacant chair next to you as a foot or leg rest, or perhaps as a resting place for your belongings. Resist the temptation! Even though that chair may be temporarily free, sooner or later, someone will want to play at a nearby machine, and they'll need that chair. You can save yourself a potentially nasty encounter if you limit yourself to one chair and one machine.

Similarly, some players "relax" in a chair without using the video poker machine. Maybe they've just finished a long playing session and feel they have "squatting rights." Or perhaps they haven't even played at that machine, but want to rest and soak up the casino atmosphere. Whatever the reason, there's really no excuse for taking up a seat at a machine if you don't intend to play. Remember that the slot and video poker areas are not for lounging, and show courtesy to fellow players by vacating your seat as soon as your gambling session is over.

Avoid Lengthy Cell Phone Conversations

While cell phones provide a great means of keeping in touch with those at home and work while spending time at the casino, we all know how annoying other people's conversations can be, especially when they're long and loud. Out of respect for other players—some of whom, like you, may be concentrating on playing strategies—put your cell phone on vibrate or silent mode when you're on the casino floor. This will keep the ringing from disturbing everyone around you. If you must answer the call then and there, try to keep it short and sweet—and as quiet as possible. If a long conversation is necessary, be kind enough to leave the playing area.

Tip Appropriately

Tipping is very personal. While some players don't tip at all, others provide overly lavish tips, sometimes to the detriment of their budget. Keep in mind, though, that casino workers are in the service industry, and like waiters, they rely on tips for a good portion of their income. Moreover, if you plan to patronize a casino for more than a few hours, you'll probably want to create some good will among the staff, and the best way to do that is to provide tips when appropriate.

Whom should you tip? Since video poker doesn't involve dealers, you'll be tipping fewer people than the table poker or blackjack player would. However, you should think about giving gratuities to the following people:

❑ **The cocktail server.** As mentioned earlier in the book, most casinos provide free drinks as long as you keep playing. When someone brings you a drink, whether alcohol or a soda, it's usual to tip her $1 or more.

❑ **The bartender.** If you're playing at the bar, be sure to leave a tip of at least $1 per drink. Most people also give a few dollars to the bartender after winning a hand. Keep in mind that the bartender will be glad to keep an eye on your machine if you leave for a few minutes, and will let you know if there's a special promotion. Clearly, she'll be more helpful if she's receiving appropriate tips.

❑ **The custodian called in for extra work.** If you spill a drink or find a pile of cigarette ashes you want removed, be sure to tip the cleaning person at least $1.

❑ **The attendant who delivers a jackpot.** If you are lucky enough to win a jackpot, and that jackpot is hand-delivered, you'll be expected to share a little of your wealth. The size of this tip can vary widely, and should depend not only on the amount of the jackpot, but also on the amount of money you spent before your win. If you have lost more than you won, you shouldn't feel obligated to provide a tip. Be aware, though, that in most cases, a $10 or $20 gratuity is customary after receiving a jackpot of $1,000, while $20 to $40 is in order when you've won $4,000 or so. If more than one person brings the money, it's permissible to ask them to split the tip.

❑ **The casino host or hostess.** You may remember reading about the casino host—sometimes called the slot host—in Chapter 5. This is the person who can advise you of your comp status, offer discretionary comps, and perform a range of other services. Although it is not necessary, it is customary to occasionally buy your casino host a small gift, such as candy or a bottle of wine, if she has done a favor for you.

Finally, consider giving a small tip—a dollar or two—to any employee who performs an extra service for you. If a staff member is kind enough to watch your machine while you take a break or to walk you to your car after a win, a tip is definitely in order.

There is no requirement that you tip casino employees. But if you plan to spend some time on the casino floor, you may find that appropriate tipping yields good will—and good service.

Total Your Tickets Before Cashing Them In

As discussed in Chapter 2, when you finish playing at any TITO machine and you hit the *Cash Out* button, the machine will dispense a bar-coded ticket through a slot labeled "COLLECT TICKET." If the ticket shows any remaining credits, it can be exchanged for cash by the casino cashiers or at a self-redemption machine.

If after an evening or afternoon of play, you find yourself with two or more of these tickets, you'll want to avoid wasting the time of other players as well as the staff by totaling all of your tickets before handing them to the cashier. Simply insert the tickets, one after the other, in the bill validator of any slot or video poker machine, and the machine will print out a single ticket that shows your total credits. Sure, you can hand a pile of cash tickets to a cashier and have her do the extra work, but with a bit more effort on your part, you can speed the process along for everyone concerned.

Don't Take "Forbidden" Items Onto the Casino Floor

Years ago, players were strictly forbidden to take photos on the casino floor. On one hand, some gamblers didn't want to be photographed. On the other, the casino didn't want potential cheaters to receive information that would allow them to unfairly win games. For this reason, players were prohibited from taking cameras and cell phones with cameras into the casino.

Now, because it is simply too difficult to prevent people from carrying cell phones, many casinos have relaxed their rules regarding cameras—although the rules are still strictly enforced in European casinos. The bottom line is that you will probably be allowed to take your cell phone with camera onto the casino floor, but it is wise to avoid using its camera capabilities until you've left the premises.

In earlier chapters, I explained that electronic devices of all kinds are likely to draw the attention of the casino staff, whether they see the device directly or it's picked up by one of the surveillance cameras. Casinos are afraid that these devices can be programmed to give you an advantage while playing. For this reason, if you are seen using a Palm Pilot, a laptop computer, a calculator, or any other electronic gadget, a casino employee will either ask you to put it away or tell you to leave the casino.

Occasionally, a casino employee asks to see my video poker strategy cards. After looking at the cards, though, she always allows me to use them because unlike electronic devices, strategy cards are not forbidden.

CASINO SAFETY

Casinos do their best to protect both themselves and their players through the use of surveillance cameras and a trained security force. But whenever money is involved—especially large sums of money—there are bound to be unscrupulous people looking for easy cash. And, of course, even the most massive security system can't protect every player at every moment. That's why it's important to do all that you can to ensure your own safety, as well as the safety of your money and other valuables.

Take a Minimum of Cash and Other Valuables Onto the Casino Floor

The process of safeguarding your valuables should actually begin at home, rather than the casino, and should start with a paring-down process. Before leaving on vacation, go through your wallet and pull out any credit cards or ATM cards you won't need, and put them in a safe place. That way, you won't have to worry about them while you're on the casino floor.

What's the best way to safeguard your valuables? Take only what you need onto the casino floor and leave the rest in your room safe, in the hotel safe, or—even better—at home.

Are you thinking of wearing your most stunning jewelry during evenings at the casino? Although a beautiful casino may seem like the perfect place to enjoy your best necklace and earrings, that jewelry—along with designer handbags and other high-priced accessories—is going to mark you as a potential victim. Trust me: You'll have just as much fun in the casino if you dress in a less conspicuous manner, and you'll be a whole lot safer.

Once you get to the casino, think back to Chapter 4, where I urged you to take only your bankroll for that particular gambling session to the casino floor, and to leave the rest of your cash in your room safe or, in the absence of that, the hotel safe. This will not only help you stick to your budget, but will also keep most of your cash away from the prying eyes and fast hands of would-be thieves. Any jewelry you're not wearing should also be kept in the safe.

Keep Your Eye on Your Possessions

No matter how much you pare down your valuables before entering the casino, you'll probably be carrying a wallet, a handbag, or both.

Keep these items not just near you but *on* you as you play. Men should carry wallets in a front pocket rather than a back one, as a deterrent to pickpockets. If possible, they should wear a shirt with buttoned pockets and keep their wallet there, making it impossible for the pickpocket to reach it. Women should at all times keep their pocketbooks wrapped around a shoulder or set in their lap. In no case should you place a purse or other valuables on a free chair or in the space between the machines. This is tantamount to an invitation to a thief—especially if there's a pass-through between the machine you're using and the bank of machines behind it. It's all too easy for someone to stick her hand through the space and grab your belongings.

Avoid Leaving Your Video Poker Machine Unattended

If you absolutely must leave your machine for a few moments and want to make sure that someone can't easily cash out your credits, push the Deal/Draw *button before stepping away. This will make it impossible for a thief to cash out before the new hand has been played.*

We've already discussed how it's bad manners to leave the machine you're playing for a long period of time, with the intention of resuming play. Good machines are usually in scarce supply, and it's simply inconsiderate to place one on "hold." But this practice is also unwise from a safety perspective. More than once, I've seen people watch a machine until the player leaves for a break, and then start playing on the first person's credits. Some thieves are even brazen enough to immediately cash out the player's credits. That's why it makes sense to keep your eye on your machine at all times, and to cash out if you plan to take more than a short break. Remember that it takes only a moment for someone to press a button and make away with your hard-earned money.

Be Careful With Your Winnings

A surprising number of players walk away from the cashier's cage with their winnings in their hands. I urge you to take the time to first count your money, and then put your money in your purse or wallet before walking away from the cage. There's no need to advertise your win by exhibiting a stack of bills.

If you decide to use a self-redemption machine to cash your credits, note that the cash is sometimes dispensed in two packets instead of one. This makes it even more important to count your money before stepping away from the machine. If you don't, the next person in line may end up with a portion of your winnings.

If you've won a jackpot—especially a large hand-paid jackpot—be aware that the commotion will make your good fortune known to everyone in that area of the casino. For this reason, it's smart to enlist some help in getting your cash to a safe place. If you are a guest of the casino, ask the staff to keep the money in a safe deposit box for the remainder of your stay. Most casinos make this service available to their guests. If you are staying at another hotel, ask security to escort you to your car or taxi to make sure you get there safely. Better yet, ask the casino if you can have a check instead of cash, and avoid the problem of getting a pile of bills to your room or vehicle. Although casinos are usually not willing to convert separate small wins into a check, they will provide a major jackpot in check form.

> If you drive to the casino, take advantage of valet parking. One or two dollars is a small price to pay for safety—especially since many casino parking lots are poorly lit.

Be Aware of the People Around You

One of the best ways you can keep yourself safe is to remain aware of any suspicious behavior on the part of those around you. Keep an eye open for anyone who is watching you as you play at a machine, or following you either within or outside the casino. If you feel that someone is paying undue attention to you, don't hesitate to contact security. They will be just as eager as you are to eliminate that person from the casino because the last thing they want is a reputation for being unsafe.

Although thieves have been known to steal money and other valuables on a busy casino floor—in front of both a crowd of people and the eye of the security camera—you'll want to be even more careful when entering an elevator on casino property. Never get into an elevator with someone who makes you feel nervous. Instead, trust your instincts and wait for a different car.

> Most casinos keep a list of "undesirables," and ban known thieves from entering casino property. But while security staff is good at spotting repeat offenders, they are most effective when players bring any suspicious behavior to their attention.

Immediately Report Losses of Money and Other Valuables

Despite your best efforts, your wallet, pocketbook, or other valuables may be lost or stolen during your casino stay. As soon as you notice the loss, be sure to report it to security. If you've misplaced an item like a jacket or driver's license, there's a good chance that someone will have turned it in. Slot club cards inadvertently left in machines are also often found and turned in by the next player. The chance of seeing lost or

Casino Safety Tips

This chapter presents practical guidelines for keeping safe during your time in a casino. Because this is such an important subject, it makes sense to quickly review some safety tips.

❑ **Take only necessary items onto the casino floor.** Leave all other valuables—cash, credit cards, and jewelry—at home or in the hotel safe.

❑ **Keep your eye on your possessions while in the casino.** Keep your wallet in a front pocket—ideally, in a buttoned *shirt* pocket—and keep your purse in your hand or wrapped around your shoulder.

❑ **Keep your eye on your video poker machine.** As long as you have credits in the machine, avoid leaving it unguarded.

❑ **Be careful with your winnings.** Have your winnings converted to a check when possible, ask security to escort you to your car, or request that the casino keep your money in a safe. *Never* flaunt or brag about the money you've won.

❑ **Be alert to your surroundings.** Is someone following you or watching you as you play? If so, contact casino security.

❑ **Quickly report any property losses.** Let casino security know about lost cash and other valuables. If you're lucky, the surveillance camera will lead them to your property.

stolen money, credit cards, and jewelry, however, is not as good. If you're lucky, security will be able to find both the thief and your possessions by checking the casino's security cameras. If not, consider it a lesson learned and be more careful next time.

IN CONCLUSION

The majority of people who frequent a casino are good citizens, just like you. But it takes only one unscrupulous person to turn your casino vacation into a nightmare. By using commonsense precautions and remaining alert to your surroundings, you'll be able to return home safe and sound, with only good memories of your trip.

CONCLUSION

I f you have read and absorbed the material presented in this book, you're probably eager to visit a casino and start playing video poker. But don't be so impatient that you fail to take the steps necessary to get the video poker edge. In order to fully enjoy the casino experience, to make your bankroll last a long time, and, hopefully, to come home with some winnings, you'll want to make sure to do the following:

❏ Decide on the video poker games you're going to play, and practice playing them at home using the strategy tables found in Chapter 3.

❏ Decide on your gambling budget *before* leaving home. Then, when you get to the casino, stick to it.

❏ Don't enter a casino without your pay charts and strategy cards. You'll need them to make wise choices when selecting and playing games.

❏ Pick a casino that offers *real* video poker machines with good payouts.

❏ Whenever you enter a new casino, apply for a slot club card. Then use it each and every time you play.

❏ Use your pay charts to home in on the best-paying version of each game.

❏ Keep an eye out for progressive jackpots and promotions that can boost your winnings.

❏ Take the precautions necessary to safeguard yourself and your possessions. You want to go home with stories of games won—not of wallets and purses lost.

Finally, it's important to emphasize that video poker is not a job or a chore, but an exciting, exhilarating pursuit. Yes, you should stick to your budget and make smart decisions, but you should never lose sight of your primary goal—having fun. That's actually *why* I've urged you to use budgets and playing strategies. After all, you're not going to have a great time if you lose your whole bankroll your first hour in the casino!

This book has provided you with all the information you need to gain the video poker edge. The rest is up to you. I look forward to seeing you in the casinos.

GLOSSARY

action. The amount of money wagered in a video poker machine during a session, a day, or a trip. This is one factor used to determine comps and cash back by some casinos.

advantage players. Video poker players who look for the best expected returns available and rely on mathematically sound strategies rather than luck to guide their play.

ante. In table poker, a forced bet put in the pot before the cards are dealt.

auto hold. Virtual cards on the screen of a video poker machine that are automatically held by the machine. This can occur to save a winning hand, to instruct the player, or because the machine is a video lottery terminal.

bankroll. The amount of money allotted for gambling by a player.

Bet Down button. The button on the pay table page of the video poker machine that highlights the payout column results as you decrease your bet.

Bet Max button. The button on a video poker machine that allows you to bet the maximum coins for that game—usually, five coins. This is sometimes labeled Play Max Credits or Play 5 Credits.

Bet One Credit button. The button on a video poker machine that allows you to bet one coin at a time.

Bet Up button. The button on the pay table page of the video poker machine that highlights the payout column results as you increase your bet.

bill acceptor. The assembly on a video poker machine that accepts valid paper currency or cash tickets, and issues credit in return.

bonus. Extra money paid for a specific hand.

bounceback cash. Extra money given to players as an incentive to play at that casino.

call attendant. A message displayed on the screen of a video poker machine indicating that assistance is needed from a casino staff member.

candle. A cylindrical light found on top of a video poker machine indicating that a jackpot was hit or that service is needed.

card reader slot. The slot on a video poker machine that allows you to insert a slot club card.

cash back. Money given to a player by a casino as an incentive to play at that casino.

Cash Out button. The button on a video poker machine that allows you to collect cash or a cash ticket for any credits remaining in the machine after play.

cash ticket. *See* ticket voucher.

cashier. The casino employee who converts coins and chips into currency and conducts other financial transactions.

casino advantage game. A game with an expected

return of less than 100%, which therefore favors the casino rather than the player. This is also called a negative game.

casino host or hostess. The casino staff member assigned to assist frequent players. This person can offer "discretionary comps"—comps that are not deducted from the player's comp account.

Change button. *See* Change/Call Attendant button.

Change/Call Attendant button. The button on a video poker machine that lets the casino staff know that the player needs service. In newer machines, this is a red button labeled Change.

club card. *See* slot club card.

coin slot. The opening found in older video poker machines in which coins can be inserted for play.

coin-in. The total amount of money bet by a player in a video poker machine during a session, a day, or a trip.

cold machine. A video poker machine that isn't paying well.

cold streak. A run of losing hands.

commercial casino. A casino that is operated in a state-regulated jurisdiction, and therefore must use video poker machines that deal random card sequences, follow state mandates regarding minimum and maximum expected returns, and pay a state gaming tax. In this book, the term "commercial casino" is usually used to refer to a land-based commercial casino rather than a riverboat casino.

comp. Short for "complimentary," a reward provided by a casino as an incentive to play at that casino. Comps can include free meals, hotel room, show tickets, merchandise, and other incentives. *See also* marketing comp.

comp card. *See* slot club card.

comp status. *See* rating.

consecutive cards. A sequence of cards with no gaps or spaces between them.

credits. The record of coins remaining in a video poker machine as the result of play. Credits can be cashed in for money.

cruise ship casino. A casino found on a commercial cruise ship. Because they float in international waters, these casinos do not have to follow state mandates, but are supposed to follow the guidelines set by the International Council of Cruise Lines.

Currency Transaction Report (CTR). A report that must be filed by a casino when a player wins $10,000 or more.

Deal/Draw button. The button on a video poker machine that triggers play, causing the initial hand of cards to be shown on the video display screen.

dedicated machine. A video poker machine that offers only one game.

denomination. The value of each "coin" played in a particular video poker game—a penny, nickel, quarter, dollar, etc.

discard. A card in a dealt hand that the player chooses to replace in an effort to improve his hand.

discretionary comp. A free meal, gift, room, show ticket, or other incentive provided by a casino that doesn't reduce the player's comp account.

Double Down button. The button on a video poker machine touch screen that allows you to play for double or nothing when you have a winning hand.

downgrade. The changing of a pay table of a video poker machine from one with a higher expected return to one with a lower expected return.

edge. A competitive advantage, usually expressed as a percentage.

ER. *See* expected return.

EV. *See* expected value.

even money. A payoff that is equal to the amount wagered.

expected return (ER). The theoretical return a player can expect from a specific video poker game if he plays it correctly for a long period of time. Expressed as a percentage, this is also referred to as a payback percentage.

expected value (EV). The amount of money a player should be ahead after playing a positive (player advantage) game for a specific amount of time. This figure is based on both the game's expected return and the amount being wagered.

eye in the sky. Common term for a casino's camera surveillance system, which is located in the ceiling and records activity on the casino floor.

face card. A Jack, Queen, or King. This is also called a picture card.

five and five dealing. A method of dealing—used by video poker machines made after 1996—in which the machine chooses only the five cards of the initial hand at the draw. The machine then resumes continuous shuffling until the player pushes the Deal/Draw button.

Five of a Kind. Five cards of the same value or rank, achieved by using one or more wild cards.

flea. A term used by casino management to describe the low roller advantage player, who is considered annoying but no threat to the bottom line.

Flush. Five cards of the same suit, not in consecutive order.

fold. In table poker, the act of exiting the game and forfeiting all money so far placed in the pot.

Four Flush. Four cards of the same suit that need an additional card of that suit to make a Flush.

Four of a Kind. Four cards of the same value or rank.

Four Straight. Four cards that require an additional card to make a Straight.

Full House. Three cards of the same value or rank plus two cards of another value or rank.

full-pay game. The version of a specific game that will give you the best possible return on your bet.

gaffed. Rigged or fixed. This term is used to describe a video poker machine that has been tampered with.

gambling junket. A package set up for groups of gamblers who are considered special guests of the hotel. Junkets for high rollers can include free chartered jet service, limousines, hotel room, food, and beverages.

gap. A space in a sequence of cards that must be filled in order to make a consecutive sequence.

gut-shot. Slang term for a card that is needed to complete an Inside Four-Straight.

handle. The amount of money put through a video poker machine. Casino executives use this information to make pay table decisions.

hand-paid jackpot. A video poker jackpot so large that it is delivered to the player by a casino employee.

Help button. The button on a video poker machine touch screen that prompts the machine to display the rules of a particular game.

high cards. In most games, the Ace, King, Queen, and Jack. In some games, though, the high cards also include Nine and Ten.

high pair. A paying pair for a particular game.

high roller. A gambler who has a large bankroll and plays for large stakes.

hold percentage. The casino's theoretical take, which is important in determining comps and cash back.

Hold/Cancel button. The button on a video poker machine that causes the machine to hold (keep) that card, rather than discard it.

hopper. The receptacle inside older video poker machines in which coins are collected.

host. *See* casino host or hostess.

hot machine. A machine that is paying well.

hot streak. A run of winning hands.

house. A casino.

Inside Four-Straight. A broken sequence of four cards that requires one card to make a Straight.

jackpot. A large payout. *See also* progressive jackpot.

junket. *See* gambling junket.

kicker. In certain video poker games, a particular card that is rewarded with extra money.

kiosk. A computer terminal located in a casino that allows players to conduct slot club business without waiting in line.

land-based commercial casino. *See* commercial casino.

long run. A large number of hands that must be played in order for the actual results of a game to closely resemble that game's expected return.

low cards. In most games, the number cards—Two, Three, Four, Five, Six, Seven, Eight, Nine, and Ten. In some games, though, Nine and Ten are considered high cards.

low pair. A nonpaying pair for a particular game.

low roller. A gambler who has a small bankroll and plays for small stakes.

marketing comp. An offer of a free product, room, or other incentive that comes in the mail to the member of a slot club, and should not reduce the player's comp account.

More Games button. The button on a video poker machine touch screen that causes a menu of games to be displayed on the screen.

multi-game video poker machine. A video poker machine that offers several different games.

multi-hand video poker machine. A video poker machine that allows you to play from one to a hundred hands of the same game at the same time. This is also called a multi-play or multi-line machine.

multi-line video poker machine. See multi-hand video poker machine.

multi-play video poker machine. See multi-hand video poker machine.

Native American Indian casino. A casino owned and run by a government-recognized Native American tribe that is considered a sovereign entity, and has made an individual pact with the government of the state in which it is located. This is also called a tribal casino.

natural hand. A winning hand that contains no wild cards.

negative game. See casino advantage game.

noncasino retailer. In this book, a retail business such as a bar, restaurant, or convenience store that offers electronic gambling devices such as video poker and slots. Most of the video poker machines found in these venues are video lottery terminals. See video lottery terminal.

online casino. A casino found only on the Internet. These casinos are all operated from outside the United States, and are unregulated by the United States Government.

Open-Ended Four Straight. Four consecutive cards that need either one of two cards—one at either end of the sequence—to make a Straight.

Pair. Two cards of the same value or rank.

parallel dealing. A method of dealing—used by video poker machines made before the mid-eighties—in which the machine simultaneously chooses not just the five cards of the initial hand, but also the five replacement cards, assigning each of the five replacement cards to one of the original draw cards. When a player discards a card, the assigned replacement card is revealed.

parimutuel. A racetrack.

pat hand. A dealt hand in which the player keeps all his cards without drawing new cards.

pay chart. An abbreviated version of a pay table that shows not only how many coins are returned for each winning hand based on coins bet for a particular game, but also the game's expected return.

pay table. A table, found on every video poker machine, that shows how many coins are returned for each winning hand based on the number of coins bet.

payback percentage. See expected return.

penalty card. A card in a dealt hand that if discarded will reduce the player's chance of drawing a Flush or a Straight.

perk. Short for "perquisite," a reward provided by a casino to a player as an incentive to play at that casino. Perks can include a complimentary room, food, and beverages; promotional gifts; cash back; show tickets; and more.

picture card. See face card.

Play 5 Credits button. See Bet Max button.

Play Max Credits button. See Bet Max button.

player advantage game. A game with an expected return of more than 100%, which therefore favors the player rather than the casino. This is also called a positive game.

players club. *See* slot club.

players club card. *See* slot club card.

points. *See* slot club points.

positive game. *See* player advantage game.

progressive game. A game played at a video poker machine that's linked with other machines, all of which feed a progressive jackpot. *See* progressive jackpot.

progressive jackpot. A monetary payout for a specific winning hand—usually, a Royal Flush—that increases until a player wins the jackpot.

quicket. *See* ticket voucher.

racino. A racetrack that offers electronic gaming, such as video poker and slots. Most of the video poker machines found in these venues are video lottery terminals.

random number generator (RNG). The internal component of a video poker machine that, through use of a computer chip, produces random combinations of numbers, each of which represents a specific card.

rank. The numerical value of a playing card.

rating. The casino's evaluation of a player's level of comps. This is also called comp status.

Return to Game button. The button on a video poker machine touch screen that allows you to start playing once you have decided on your game and wager.

RFB. A comp level at which a player receives free room, food, and beverages.

RFBL. A comp level at which a player receives limited room, food, and beverages.

RFL. A comp level at which a player receives name-brand liquor as well as upgraded room and food. This is a higher comp level than RFB or RFBL.

risk of ruin. The likelihood that a player will exhaust his bankroll.

riverboat casino. A commercial casino located on a body of water, although no longer required to cruise. Considered commercial casinos, riverboat casinos must follow state mandates. But because they must pay higher taxes than land-based casinos, riverboat casinos generally offer lower expected returns than their land-based counterparts.

RNG. *See* random number generator.

Royal Cycle. The approximate number of hands it takes to get a Royal Flush. For most video poker games, this is about 40,000 hands.

Royal Flush. An Ace, King, Queen, Jack, and Ten of the same suit.

See Pays button. The button on a video poker machine touch screen that causes the machine to display the game's pay table, as well as virtual buttons that allow you to highlight the amount you want to bet.

Sequential Royal Flush. A Royal Flush that appears on the screen of the video poker machine in perfect ascending or descending order, instead of random order. Extra money is sometimes paid for this rare hand.

serial dealing. A method of dealing—used by video poker machines made between the mid-eighties and late nineties—in which the machine simultaneously chooses not just the five cards of the initial hand, but also the five replacement cards, and stacks the replacements sequentially. When a player discards a card, the first replacement card in the sequence is revealed.

short-coin bet. A bet of less than maximum coins.

slot card. *See* slot club card.

slot club. A club created by a casino to promote customer loyalty by offering complimentary services, such as free rooms and meals, as an incentive to play at that casino.

slot club card. A card, issued by a casino, that when inserted in a video poker machine, allows the casino to track your play and reward you with complimentary services such as free meals, free rooms, etc. This is sometimes known as a slot card, players club card, club card, or comp card.

slot club points. Points issued by slot clubs to members of the club as an incentive to play at that casino. The points are based on the amount of money wagered over time, and can be redeemed for benefits such as cash, meals, and merchandise.

Speed button. The button on a video poker machine touch screen that modifies the speed with which the machine deals the cards.

Straight. Five cards of more than one suit in consecutive order.

Straight Flush. Five cards of the same suit in consecutive order.

suit. One of four possible categories of playing cards: hearts, diamonds, spades, or clubs.

suited. Of the same suit.

theo. Short for "theoretical loss," the theoretical amount of money a casino expects to profit from an individual's play. This amount is used to determine the player's comps.

Three of a Kind. Three cards of the same value or rank.

ticket acceptor. The assembly on a video poker machine that accepts a cash ticket and issues credit in return.

ticket voucher. The ticket dispensed by newer video poker machines (ticket-in ticket-out machines) that can be exchanged for cash by the casino cashier or at a self-redemption machine. This voucher is also called a quicket and a cash ticket.

ticket-in ticket-out (TITO) machine. A video poker machine that accepts currency or a cash ticket in return for credit, and dispenses a paper ticket voucher rather than coins when the player cashes out.

TITO machine. *See* ticket-in ticket-out machine.

toke. Slang term for a tip given to casino staff.

touch screen. A screen on a new video poker machine that provides virtual buttons on the screen, in addition to the physical buttons located below the screen,

and enables players to hold a card by touching its image.

tournament. *See* video poker tournament.

tribal casino. *See* Native American Indian casino.

Two Pair. Two cards of one value or rank, plus two cards of another value or rank.

validation decal. A sticker on the outside of a video poker machine indicating that the machine has been legally installed.

variance. A measure of the volatility of the game. Variance indicates how far actual game results will tend to deviate from expected results in the short term. *See also* volatility.

video display screen. The portion of a video poker machine on which the virtual cards appear, along with certain virtual buttons.

video lottery terminal (VLT). An electronic game machine that looks like a video poker machine, but instead is programmed to produce a certain number of winners, like a paper lottery. Most VLTs do not contain random number generators (RNGs) and do not require skill or strategy.

video poker tournament. A contest, set up by a casino, in which players compete for cash prizes.

volatility. The likelihood that, while playing a game, any individual result will vary greatly from the expected return. In high volatility games, short-term results are likely to vary from the expected return. In low volatility games, short-term results are likely to be close to the expected return. *See also* variance.

wager. The amount bet on a game.

wild card. A card that can represent any other card in order to complete a hand.

win/loss statement. A statement issued by a casino showing a player's total amount won or lost for a particular year. This statement can reflect only that gaming activity which has been tracked through the use of a slot club card.

W-2G form. A tax form issued by a casino when a player wins a single jackpot of $1,200 or more. Copies are given to the player and filed with the IRS.

PAY CHARTS FOR COMMON VIDEO POKER GAMES

Chapter 3 presents pay charts for different versions of the eight games recommended in this book. Because you may at some time want to play video poker games other than those eight, on the following pages, I have included pay charts for a number of popular games that you are sure to see in casinos, as well as for the games I've recommended. Although you should ideally stick to the full-pay versions of the eight games I endorse, I do feel that, should you decide to try your hand at a different game, it's important to know what the expected returns are so that you can choose the best version possible. These charts provide some of the important information needed to make smart decisions on the casino floor. But before you bet money on any of these games, I urge you to learn its hand rankings, to find proven strategies for playing the game, and to *practice* those strategies at home.

Just like the pay charts provided on pages 54 to 56, the following charts first list the per-coin return for both 1-coin and 5-coin wagers. Following this, you'll find the expected return (ER) for each game. Finally, I have noted whether that version of the game is a *full-pay* version—the best-paying version you are likely to find in casinos. Be aware that I've listed some versions that have even higher ERs than the full-pay game. Unfortunately, these versions can be found only rarely. When and if you do come across one, though, you'll want to take advantage of the opportunity.

You may be surprised to find that some of the games I don't recommend are positive. That is, they have an ER of over 100%, and therefore give the player the advantage. Why, then, don't I encourage you to play games such as All American Poker or Deuces Deluxe? These are not among my suggested games because they are very hard to find, and in many cases are either difficult to play correctly or have high volatility. Therefore, they do not meet the criteria that I used to select the games discussed throughout this book.

Finally, please note that in some cases, I have used the margin of the page to provide either the manufacturer's name or the commonly used player's name of the game. Just keep in mind that when trying to locate a specific game, you should not rely solely on names but should carefully match up the pay table on the video poker machine with that on your pay chart.

Pay Charts for Common Video Poker Games

Aces and Faces		
Coin Payoffs	**Expected Return***	**Best Game? (Full Pay)**
1 coin: 1-2-3-4-5-8-25-40-80-50-250 5 coins: 5-10-15-20-25-40-125-200-400-250-4000	99.26%	Yes
All American Poker		
Coin Payoffs	**Expected Return***	**Best Game? (Full Pay)**
1 coin: 1-1-3-8-8-8-30-200-250 5 coins: 5-5-15-40-40-40-150-1000-4000	98.49%	No
1 coin: 1-1-3-8-8-8-40-200-250 5 coins: 5-5-15-40-40-40-200-1000-4000	100.72%	Yes
Bonus Poker		
Coin Payoffs	**Expected Return***	**Best Game? (Full Pay)**
1 coin: 1-1-3-5-7-10-25-40-80-50-250 5 coins: 5-5-15-25-35-50-125-200-400-250-4000	92.54%	No
1 coin: 1-1-3-5-8-10-25-40-80-50-250 5 coins: 5-5-15-25-40-50-125-200-400-250-4000	94.18%	No
1 coin: 1-2-3-4-5-6-25-40-80-50-250 5 coins: 5-10-15-20-25-30-125-200-400-250-4000	96.87%	No
1 coin: 1-2-3-4-5-7-25-40-80-50-250 5 coins: 5-10-15-20-25-35-125-200-400-250-4000	98.01%	No
1 coin: 1-2-3-4-5-8-30-30-30-50-250 5 coins: 5-10-15-20-25-40-150-150-150-250-4000	98.48%	No
1 coin: 1-2-3-4-5-8-25-40-80-50-250 5 coins: 5-10-15-20-25-40-125-200-400-250-4000	99.17%	Yes

Bonus Poker Deluxe		
Coin **Payoffs**	**Expected** **Return***	**Best Game?** **(Full Pay)**
1 coin: 1-1-3-4-5-7-80-50-250 5 coins: 5-5-15-20-25-35-400-250-4000	96.25%	No
1 coin: 1-1-3-4-5-8-80-50-250 5 coins: 5-5-15-20-25-40-400-250-4000	97.40%	No
1 coin: 1-1-3-4-6-8-80-50-250 5 coins: 5-5-15-20-30-40-400-250-4000	98.49%	No
1 coin: 1-1-3-4-6-9-80-50-250 5 coins: 5-5-15-20-30-45-400-250-4000	99.64%	Yes

Deuces Wild			
Coin **Payoffs**	**Expected** **Return***	**Best Game?** **(Full Pay)**	
1 coin: 1-2-2-3-4-10-15-25-200-250 5 coins: 5-10-10-15-20-50-75-125-1000-4000	94.82%	No	Players refer to this game as Coyote Ugly.
1 coin: 1-2-2-3-4-13-16-25-200-250 5 coins: 5-10-10-15-20-65-80-125-1000-4000	96.77%	No	This game is commonly referred to as Colorado Deuces.
1 coin: 1-2-3-4-4-10-12-20-200-250 5 coins: 5-10-15-20-20-50-60-100-1000-4000	97.58%	No	Manufacturers call this game Deuces Wild.
1 coin: 1-2-2-3-4-10-15-25-400-250 5 coins: 5-10-10-15-20-50-75-125-2000-4000	98.86%	No	The manufacturer's name for this game is Double Deuces.
1 coin: 1-2-3-4-4-9-15-25-200-250 5 coins: 5-10-15-20-20-45-75-125-1000-4000	98.91%	No	Players refer to this game as either Illinois Deuces or Airport Deuces.
1 coin: 1-2-2-3-4-11-16-25-200-250 5 coins: 5-10-10-15-20-55-80-125-2000-4000	99.62%	Yes	The manufacturer's name for this game is Double Deuces.
1 coin: 1-2-3-4-4-10-16-25-200-250 5 coins: 5-10-15-20-20-50-80-125-1000-4000	99.73%	Yes	The common player's name for this game is Not-So-Ugly Deuces Wild.
1 coin: 1-2-2-3-4-8-10-20-600-250 5 coins: 5-10-10-15-20-40-50-100-3000-4000	99.92%	No	The manufacturer calls this game Triple Deuces.
1 coin: 1-2-3-4-4-11-15-25-200-250 5 coins: 5-10-15-20-20-55-75-125-1000-4000	99.96%	No	
1 coin: 1-2-2-3-4-8-15-25-500-250 5 coins: 5-10-10-15-20-40-75-125-2500-4000	100.15%	Yes	The manufactuer refers to this game as Loose Deuces.
1 coin: 1-2-2-3-5-9-15-25-200-250 5 coins: 5-10-10-15-25-45-75-125-1000-4000	100.76%	Yes	Players commonly call this game Full-Pay Deuces Wild.
1 coin: 1-2-2-3-4-13-16-25-400-250 5 coins: 5-10-10-15-20-65-80-125-2000-4700	100.92%	Better than full pay, but rare.	The common name for this game is Downtown Deuces.

Players call this game
Sam's Town Deuces.

Coin Payoffs	Expected Return*	Best Game? (Full Pay)
1 coin: 1-2-3-4-4-10-10-20-400-250 5 coins: 5-10-15-20-20-50-50-100-2000-4000	100.95%	Better than full pay, but rare.
1 coin: 1-2-2-3-5-9-15-25-200-250 5 coins: 5-10-10-15-25-45-75-125-1000-4000	101.28%	Better than full pay, but rare.**

Bonus Deuces		
Coin Payoffs	Expected Return*	Best Game? (Full Pay)
1 coin: 1-1-2-3-4-12-20-40-80-25-200-400-250 5 coins: 5-5-10-15-20-60-100-200-400-125-1000-2000-4000	96.22%	No
1 coin: 1-1-2-3-4-13-20-40-80-25-200-400-250 5 coins: 5-5-10-15-20-65-100-200-400-125-1000-2000-4000	96.71%	No
1 coin: 1-1-2-3-4-9-20-50-160-20-200-400-250 5 coins: 5-5-10-15-20-45-100-250-800-100-1000-2000-4000	97.68%	No
1 coin: 1-1-3-3-4-13-20-40-80-25-200-400-250 5 coins: 5-5-15-15-20-65-100-200-400-125-1000-2000-4000	98.80%	No
1 coin: 1-1-3-4-4-9-20-40-80-25-200-400-250 5 coins: 5-5-15-20-20-45-100-200-400-125-1000-2000-4000	99.45%	Yes
1 coin: 1-1-3-4-4-10-20-40-80-25-200-400-250 5 coins: 5-5-15-20-20-50-100-200-400-125-1000-2000-4000	99.86%	Better than full pay, but rare.

Deuces Deluxe		
Coin Payoffs	Expected Return*	Best Game? (Full Pay)
1 coin: 1-2-3-4-4-9-10-15-25-50-200-250 5 coins: 5-10-15-20-20-45-75-125-250-1000-4000	100.32%	Yes

Super Bonus Deuces		
Coin Payoffs	Expected Return*	Best Game? (Full Pay)
1 coin: 1-2-2-3-4-6-8-20-160-200-400-250 5 coins: 5-10-10-15-20-30-40-100-800-1000-2000-4000	95.61%	No
1 coin: 1-2-2-3-4-8-10-20-160-200-400-250 5 coins: 5-10-10-15-20-40-50-100-800-1000-2000-4000	96.94%	No
1 coin: 1-2-2-3-4-8-10-25-160-200-400-250 5 coins: 5-10-10-15-20-40-50-125-800-1000-2000-4000	97.87%	No
1 coin: 1-2-2-3-4-9-12-25-160-200-400-250 5 coins: 5-10-10-15-20-45-60-125-800-1000-2000-4000	98.89%	Yes
1 coin: 1-2-2-3-4-9-15-25-160-200-400-250 5 coins: 5-10-10-15-20-45-75-125-800-1000-2000-4000	99.67%	Better than full pay, but rare.

Double Bonus Poker		
Coin Payoffs	**Expected Return***	**Best Game? (Full Pay)**
1 coin: 1-1-3-4-5-6-50-80-160-50-250 5 coins: 5-5-15-20-25-30-250-400-800-4000	92.04%	No
1 coin: 1-1-3-4-5-8-50-80-160-50-250 5 coins: 5-5-15-20-25-40-250-400-800-4000	94.19%	No
1 coin: 1-1-3-4-6-9-50-80-160-50-250 5 coins: 5-5-15-20-30-45-250-400-800-4000	96.38%	No
1 coin: 1-1-3-4-7-9-50-80-160-50-250 5 coins: 5-5-15-20-35-45-250-400-800-4000	97.74%	No
1 coin: 1-1-3-4-7-10-50-80-160-50-250 5 coins: 5-5-15-20-35-50-250-400-800-4000	98.81%	No
1 coin: 1-1-3-5-6-10-50-80-160-50-250 5 coins: 5-5-15-25-30-50-250-400-800-250-4000	98.88%	No
1 coin: 1-1-3-5-7-9-50-80-160-50-250 5 coins: 5-5-15-25-35-45-250-400-800-4000	99.11%	No
1 coin: 1-1-3-5-7-10-50-80-160-50-250 5 coins: 5-5-15-25-35-50-250-400-800-4000	100.17%	Yes
Double Double Bonus Poker		
Coin Payoffs	**Expected Return***	**Best Game? (Full Pay)**
1 coin: 1-1-3-4-5-6-50-80-160-160-400-50-250 5 coins: 5-5-15-20-25-30-250-400-800-800-2000-250-4000	94.66%	No
1 coin: 1-1-3-4-5-7-50-80-160-160-400-50-250 5 coins: 5-5-15-20-25-35-250-400-800-800-2000-250-4000	95.71%	No
1 coin: 1-1-3-4-5-8-50-80-160-160-400-50-250 5 coins: 5-5-15-20-25-40-250-400-800-800-2000-250-4000	96.79%	No
1 coin: 1-1-3-4-5-9-50-80-160-160-400-50-250 5 coins: 5-5-15-20-25-45-250-400-800-800-2000-250-4000	97.87%	No
1 coin: 1-1-3-4-6-9-50-80-160-160-320-50-250 5 coins: 5-5-15-20-30-45-250-400-800-800-1600-250-4000	98.49%	No
1 coin: 1-1-3-4-6-9-50-80-160-160-400-50-250 5 coins: 5-5-15-20-30-45-250-400-800-800-2000-250-4000	98.98%	Yes
1 coin: 1-1-3-4-6-10-50-80-160-160-400-40-250 5 coins: 5-5-15-20-30-50-250-400-800-800-2000-200-4000	99.96%	Better than full pay, but rare.

Double Double Jackpot		
Coin Payoffs	**Expected Return***	**Best Game? (Full Pay)**
1 coin: 1-1-3-4-5-8-50-80-160-160-320-50-250 5 coins: 5-5-15-20-25-40-250-400-800-800-1600-250-4000	96.77%	No
1 coin: 1-1-3-4-5-9-50-80-160-160-320-50-250 5 coins: 5-5-15-20-25-45-250-400-800-800-1600-250-4000	97.86%	No
1 coin: 1-1-3-5-5-8-50-80-160-160-320-50-250 5 coins: 5-5-15-25-25-40-250-400-800-800-1600-250-4000	98.20%	No
1 coin: 1-1-3-5-6-9-50-80-160-160-320-50-250 5 coins: 5-5-15-25-30-45-250-400-800-800-1600-250-4000	100.35%	Yes

Jacks or Better		
Coin Payoffs	**Expected Return***	**Best Game? (Full Pay)**
1 coin: 1-2-3-4-5-6-25-50-250 5 coins: 5-10-15-20-25-30-125-250-4000	95.00%	No
1 coin: 1-2-3-4-5-7-25-50-250 5 coins: 5-10-15-20-25-35-125-250-4000	96.15%	No
1 coin: 1-2-3-4-5-8-25-50-250 5 coins: 5-10-15-20-25-40-125-250-4000	97.30%	No
1 coin: 1-2-3-4-6-8-25-50-250 5 coins: 5-10-15-20-30-40-125-250-4000	98.39%	No
1 coin: 1-2-3-4-5-8-30-50-250 5 coins: 5-10-15-20-25-40-150-250-4000	98.48%	No
1 coin: 1-2-3-4-6-9-25-50-250 5 coins: 5-10-15-20-30-45-125-250-4000	99.54%	Yes
1 coin: 1-2-3-4-6-9-25-50-250 5 coins: 5-10-15-20-30-45-125-250-4700	99.90%	Better than full pay, but rare.

Joker's Wild (One Joker Poker/Kings or Better)		
Coin Payoffs	**Expected Return***	**Best Game? (Full Pay)**
1 coin: 1-1-2-3-5-7-15-50-100-200-400 5 coins: 5-5-10-15-25-35-75-250-500-1000-4000	96.38%	No
1 coin: 1-1-2-3-5-7-17-50-100-200-400 5 coins: 5-5-10-15-25-35-85-250-500-1000-4000	98.09%	No
1 coin: 1-1-2-3-5-7-18-50-100-200-400 5 coins: 5-5-10-15-25-35-90-250-500-1000-4700	99.29%	No
1 coin: 1-1-2-3-5-7-20-50-100-200-400 5 coins: 5-5-10-15-25-35-100-250-500-1000-4000	100.65%	Yes

One-Eyed Jacks		
Coin Payoffs	**Expected Return***	**Best Game? (Full Pay)**
1 coin: 0-1-1-2-3-5-15-40-75-150-250 5 coins: 0-5-5-10-15-75-200-375-750-4000	96.97%	No
1 coin: 0-1-1-2-3-5-15-45-75-150-250 5 coins: 0-5-5-10-15-75-225-375-750-4000	97.95%	No
1 coin: 0-1-1-2-3-5-15-45-75-200-250 5 coins: 0-5-5-10-15-75-225-375-1000-4000	99.29%	No
1 coin: 0-1-1-2-3-5-15-50-80-180-250 5 coins: 0-5-5-10-15-75-250-400-900-4000	99.98%	Yes
1 coin: 1-1-1-2-4-5-10-50-100-100-500 5 coins: 5-5-5-10-20-50-250-500-500-8000	101.4%	Better than full pay, but rare.

Pick 'Em Poker		
Coin Payoffs	**Expected Return***	**Best Game? (Full Pay)**
1 coin: 2-3-4-10-15-18-100-50-1000 5 coins 10-15-20-50-75-90-600-250-10000	96.20%	No
1 coin: 2-3-4-10-15-18-100-200-1000 5 coins: 10-15-20-50-75-90-600-1199-6000	96.45%	No
1 coin: 2-3-4-10-15-18-100-200-1000 5 coins 10-15-20-50-75-90-600-1199-10000	96.69%	No
1 coin: 2-3-4-11-15-18-100-50-1000 5 coins 10-15-20-50-75-90-600-250-10000	96.70%	No
1 coin: 2-3-4-11-15-18-100-200-1000 5 coins: 10-15-20-55-75-90-600-1199-6000	96.95%	No
1 coin: 2-3-5-11-15-18-100-200-1000 5 coins 10-15-25-55-75-90-600-1199-6000	99.95%	Yes

Shockwave		
Coin Payoffs	**Expected Return***	**Best Game? (Full Pay)**
1 coin: 1-1-3-5-6-9-25-100-250 5 coins: 5-5-15-25-30-45-125-500-4000	93.23%	No
1 coin: 1-1-3-5-8-10-25-100-250 5 coins: 5-5-15-25-40-50-125-500-4000	97.34%	No
1 coin: 1-1-3-5-8-11-25-100-250 5 coins: 5-5-15-25-40-55-125-500-4000	98.45%	No
1 coin: 1-1-3-5-8-12-25-100-250 5 coins: 5-5-15-25-40-60-125-500-4000	99.55%	Yes, but getting rare.

Super Double Bonus Poker		
Coin Payoffs	**Expected Return***	**Best Game? (Full Pay)**
1 coin: 1-1-3-4-5-6-50-80-120-160-80-250 5 coins: 5-5-15-20-25-30-250-400-600-800-400-4000	96.87%	No
1 coin: 1-1-3-4-5-8-50-80-120-160-80-250 5 coins: 5-5-15-20-25-40-250-400-600-800-400-4000	98.69%	No
1 coin: 1-1-3-4-5-9-50-80-120-160-50-250 5 coins: 5-5-15-20-25-45-250-400-600-800-250-4000	99.37%	No
1 coin: 1-1-3-4-5-9-50-80-120-160-80-250 5 coins: 5-5-15-20-25-45-250-400-600-800-400-4000	99.69%	Yes, but getting rare.

Super Aces		
Coin Payoffs	**Expected Return***	**Best Game? (Full Pay)**
1 coin: 1-1-3-4-5-6-50-80-400-60-250 5 coins: 5-5-15-20-25-30-250-400-2000-300-4000	97.68%	No
1 coin: 1-1-3-4-5-7-50-80-400-60-250 5 coins: 5-5-15-20-25-35-250-400-2000-300-4000	98.85%	No
1 coin: 1-1-3-4-5-8-50-80-400-50-250 5 coins: 5-5-15-20-25-40-250-400-2000-250-4000	99.84%	No
1 coin: 1-1-3-4-5-8-50-80-400-60-250 5 coins: 5-5-15-20-25-40-250-400-2000-300-4000	99.94%	Yes

White Hot Aces		
Coin Payoffs	**Expected Return***	**Best Game? (Full Pay)**
1 coin: 1-1-3-4-5-7-50-120-240-50-250 5 coins: 5-5-15-20-35-250-600-1200-250-4000	97.11%	No
1 coin: 1-1-3-4-5-8-50-120-240-80-250 5 coins: 5-5-15-20-40-250-600-1200-400-4000	98.50%	No
1 coin: 1-1-3-4-5-9-50-120-240-50-250 5 coins: 5-5-15-20-45-250-600-1200-250-4000	99.24%	No
1 coin: 1-1-3-4-5-9-50-120-240-80-250 5 coins: 5-5-15-20-45-250-600-1200-400-4000	99.57%	Yes

RESOURCE LIST

This Resource List includes companies, agencies, and websites that can help you hone your video poker skills, or assist you in becoming better informed about gambling in general, or about gambling in your area of the country.

The first group of resources—Training Software and Practice Websites—guides you to proven software programs and websites that you can use to practice your video poker strategies at home.

The second group—State Regulatory Agencies—includes state websites that offer gaming rules and regulations, tribal compacts, and other technical data. In most cases, these sites also provide contact information so that you can ask specific questions about gaming in your state of interest.

Finally, you'll find General Information Groups and Agencies that offer further information about gambling in the United States, as well as help with problem gambling.

TRAINING SOFTWARE AND PRACTICE WEBSITES

Bob Dancer Products
Phone: 800-244-2224
Website: www.bobdancer.com

Bob Dancer Presents WinPoker is the most award-winning video poker software, and in my opinion, a must for practice. Fifteen templates enable you to modify the program for almost any game found in a casino.

Dan Paymar
1118 Fairgrounds Road
Farmington, NM 87401
Website: www.optimumplay.com

Paymar's *Optimum Video Poker Software* is an excellent training program with fast game analysis and the widest variety of bankroll consideration calculations. If you plan on playing video poker, this product will pay for itself in a short time.

The Frugal Gambler Store
Website: www.frugalgambler.biz

Frugal Video Poker by Wolf Gaming Software is an all-in-one video poker program, and the first to combine the play-and-learn tutorial function. It includes a twelve-minute video in which video poker expert Jean Scott explains some of the main requisites for successful video poker play. You will get more than your money's worth.

Multistrike Poker
Website: www.multistrikepoker.com

Click on "Play the Game," and try your hand at Multistrike Poker. Just keep in mind that the pay tables offered on this website are far better than those you will find in actual casinos.

STATE REGULATORY AGENCIES

Alaska Department of Revenue Gaming Unit
Website: www.tax.state.ak.us/programs/gaming/index.asp

There is limited gambling in Alaska, but this website offers revenue reports on the state's gaming industry.

Arizona Department of Gaming
Website: www.gm.state.az.us/

This website lists tribal casinos in Arizona, provides information on tribal gaming compacts, and offers other gaming-related information.

California Gambling Control Commission
Website: www.cgcc.ca.gov/

Here you'll find gaming laws and regulations, information on tribal gaming compacts, and a monthly bulletin that provides updates on gambling in California.

Colorado Division of Gaming
Website: www.gaming.state.co.us/

This site provides links to Colorado's Limited Gaming Act, monthly revenue figures for each of the three Colorado cities in which casino gaming is allowed, and relevant publications and forms.

Connecticut Division of Special Revenue
Website: www.dosr.state.ct.us/Index.html

This website offers state gaming regulations, tribal compacts, gaming statistics, and more.

Delaware Lottery Video Lottery Information Page
Website: lottery.state.de.us/videolottery.html

Visit this site for basic information about Delaware's video lottery.

Illinois Gaming Board

Website: www.igb.state.il.us/

Here is a wealth of information about riverboat gambling in Illinois, including the Riverboat Gambling Act, rules followed by the casinos, and monthly and annual revenue reports.

Indiana Gaming Commission

Website: www.state.in.us/gaming/index.html

This website presents gaming statutes and rules, as well as monthly and annual revenue reports.

Iowa Racing and Gaming Homepage

Website: www.state.ia.us/irgc/

Here you'll find information on Iowa's tribal compacts, racetrack gaming, excursion boat gaming, and more.

Kansas State Gaming Agency

Website: www.accesskansas.org/ksga/

Visit this website to learn about tribal gaming in Kansas.

Louisiana Gaming Control Board

Website: www.dps.state.la.us/lgcb/

This website offers links to information about Louisiana's racinos, land-based casinos, and riverboat gaming.

Michigan Gaming Control Board

Website: www.michigan.gov/mgcb

The Gaming Control Board website presents information about both Detroit casinos and Michigan's tribal casinos.

Minnesota Department of Public Safety

Website: www.dps.state.mn.us/alcgamb/
gamenf/gamenf.html

Visit this website to learn about tribal compacts, as well as statutes and regulations.

Mississippi Gaming Commission

Website: www.mgc.state.ms.us/

This extensive website provides regulations, in-depth monthly and quarterly reports, and other data about gaming in Mississippi.

Missouri Gaming Commission

Website: www.mgc.state.mo.us/

Here you'll find information on Missouri's riverboat casinos, including history, statutes and regulations, and financial reports.

Montana Department of Justice Gambling Control

Website: doj.state.mt.us/department/gambling
controldivision.asp

This website offers the history of gaming in Montana, as well as tribal compacts, laws and administrative rules, and statistics and reports.

Nevada Gaming Commission and State Gaming Control Board

Website: gaming.state.nv.us/

The Nevada website provides information on statutes and regulations, relevant legislation, tribal compacts, a notice on Internet wagering, and links to other important data.

New Jersey Casino Control Commission

Website: http://www.state.nj.us/casinos/

Here you'll find rules and regulations, annual reports, links to New Jersey casino information, and more.

New Mexico Gaming Control Board

Website: www.nmgcb.org/

This website provides lists of tribal casinos, offers tribal compacts, and presents gaming regulations and statutes.

New York State Racing and Wagering Board
Website: www.racing.state.ny.us

Visit this site for information on New York's tribal casinos.

North Dakota Office of Attorney, General Gaming Division
Website: http://www.ag.state.nd.us/Gaming/Gaming.htm

This website offers a sample gaming compact, provides information on North Dakota gaming laws and rules, and answers common questions on the topic.

Oregon Gaming
Website: http://www.gambling-law-us.com/State-Laws/Oregon/gaming/

Here you'll find links to information on Oregon gaming, including the Oregon lottery, gaming rules and regulations, etc.

Rhode Island Gaming
Website: http://www.gambling-law-us.com/State-Laws/Rhode-Island/gaming/

The Rhode Island Gaming website links you to information on the lottery as well as other gaming issues.

South Dakota Commission on Gaming
Website: www.state.sd.us/drr2/reg/gaming/index.htm

Visit this website for annual reports and gaming rules.

Washington State Gambling Commission
Website: www.wsgc.wa.gov/

Here you'll find rules and regulations, reports and statistics, and links to information on tribal casinos.

GENERAL INFORMATION GROUPS AND AGENCIES

American Gaming Association
555 13th Street, NW
Suite 1010 East
Washington, DC 20004
Phone: 202-637-6500
Website: http://www.americangaming.org/

This association provides detailed information about commercial casinos in the United States.

Gamblers Anonymous
PO Box 17173
Los Angeles, CA 90017
Website: www.gamblersanonymous.org/

Gamblers Anonymous offers a program and helpful information for those who wish to stop gambling,

National Indian Gaming Commission (NIGC)
1441 L Street NW
Suite 9100
Washington, DC 20005
Phone: 202-632-7003
Website: www.nigc.gov/

NIGC, an independent federal agency established to regulate and protect Indian gaming, offers a wealth of information, including the Johnson Act, the Indian Gaming Regulatory Act, lists of gaming tribes, and more.

INDEX

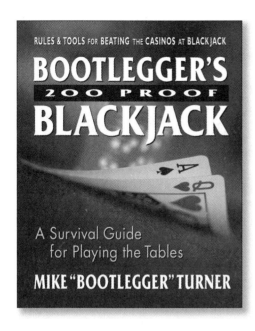

BOOTLEGGER'S 200 PROOF BLACKJACK
A Survival Guide for Playing the Tables
Mike "Bootlegger" Turner

For most of us, the game of blackjack provides excitement and entertainment—and somewhat erratic results. But hey, you started with $100, and you were prepared to stop as soon as you lost it. And that's exactly what the casinos count on. The fact is that few of us understand how to play blackjack correctly. While we may know the basic rules and even a few betting strategies, we still manage to lose our stakes over and over again. Gambling columnist and blackjack expert Mike "Bootlegger" Turner has written the perfect guide to help the average player turn the tables. *Bootlegger's 200 Proof Blackjack* provides the rules and tools for beating the casinos at their own game.

Bootlegger's 200 Proof Blackjack begins by explaining the basics of blackjack. It then examines and analyzes the most effective strategies for increasing your odds of winning. Included are discussions of money management for strategic play, tips for avoiding common pitfalls, and a unique section on using the casinos' promotional money to play. For more passionate players, the book offers easy-to-follow instructions on the best card counting systems available—the systems that casinos absolutely don't want you to know about. Throughout the book, full-color examples of card-hands illustrate and clarify plays and strategies.

If you have no problem giving the casinos your hard-earned wages, this book is not for you. But if you enjoy walking out with the casino's money, as well as your own, *Bootlegger's 200 Proof Blackjack* is the place to start your winning education.

ABOUT THE AUTHOR

Mike "Bootlegger" Turner has studied and played the game of blackjack for over thirty years. His articles on blackjack have appeared in newspapers and gambling magazines throughout North America, as well as on numerous gambling websites. Mr. Turner and his family reside in Ohio.

$17.95 • 240 pages • 7.5 x 9-inch paperback • 2-Color • ISBN 0-7570-0048-7

For more information about our books, visit our website at www.squareonepublishers.com.

FOR A COPY OF OUR CATALOG, CALL TOLL FREE 877-900-BOOK, EXT. 100

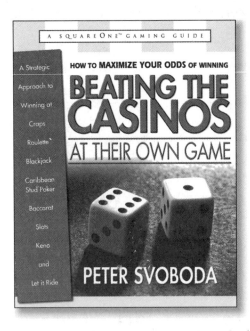

BEATING THE CASINOS AT THEIR OWN GAME

A Strategic Approach to Winning at Craps, Roulette, Blackjack, Caribbean Stud Poker, Baccarat, Slots, Keno & Let It Ride

Peter Svoboda

Beating the Casinos at Their Own Game is an easy-to-follow guide to winning at casino games. For each game, from roulette to craps and more, gambling expert Peter Svoboda first clearly explains the rules of play so that the novice gambler as well as the veteran can enter a casino with confidence. He then details the "smart" way to approach that game, including unique strategies that will increase your chance of winning. The author demonstrates which games offer the best odds, and even shows you how to manage your gambling allowance—an important key to gambling success.

With the ever-increasing popularity of Las Vegas, Atlantic City, and casinos on cruise ships and more, it's clear that the gambling industry is taking the country by storm. Now Peter Svoboda tells you not only how to get in on the action, but also how to cash in on the profits and walk away a winner.

ABOUT THE AUTHOR

Peter Svoboda is a licensed professional engineer with degrees in Mechanical and Civil Engineering from the New Jersey Institute of Technology. A veteran gambler with over twenty-five years of experience in casinos all over North America, Peter has studied the odds and probabilities of the various games to develop proven strategies of play.

$19.95 • 288 pages • 7.5 x 9-inch quality paperback • Full-Color • ISBN 0-7570-0005-3